Medication Fact Sheets

A Behavioral Medication Reference for Educators

THIRD EDITION

Dean E. Konopasek

Research Press ■ 2612 North Mattis Avenue ■ Champaign, Illinois 61822 ■ [800] 519-2707
www.researchpress.com

Originally published by Sopris West in 2003 and 2004 under the title *Medication Fact Sheets: A Behavioral Medication Reference Guide for the Education Professional.*

5   4   3   2   10   11   12   13

Copies of this book may be ordered from Research Press at the address given on the title page.

Composition by Jeff Helgesen
Cover design by Linda Brown, Positive I.D. Graphic Design, Inc.
Printed by Seaway Printing Co., Inc.

ISBN 13: 978-0-87822-618-4
Library of Congress Control Number: 2009931641

CAUTIONARY STATEMENT—IMPORTANT!

Medication Fact Sheets is designed to provide a brief overview of medications used to treat psychiatric and behavioral conditions, as well as medications for seizure disorders. As such, it provides an abbreviated description of each medication. In the interest of providing a useful general reference for nonmedical professionals in an abbreviated format, not all uses, effects, precautions, side effects, or forms of administration can be described.

This reference is specifically NOT intended as a basis for prescribing medication or as a substitute for medical advice. Questions or concerns about the need for, effects, side effects, precautions, or dosage of any medication described in *Medication Fact Sheets* should be referred to the prescribing physician or other health care professional.

Contents

Asterisked medications are no longer available under a brand name.

Introduction

In 1937, the *American Journal of Psychiatry* published an article by Charles Bradley titled "The Behavior of Children Receiving Benzedrine," describing the paradoxical calming effect the stimulant drug had on disruptive behavior we now associate with attention-deficit/hyperactivity disorder (ADHD). With publication of that article, Bradley ushered in a new era of treatment for psychiatric disorders. Since then, the use of medications in the treatment of psychiatric conditions in people across all age groups has increased steadily, if not dramatically, particularly over the past two decades. What was once a specialty treatment area limited to the field of psychiatry for patients suffering from serious mental illnesses is now an area in which general practitioners, pediatricians, and many other health care providers routinely prescribe, across a wider spectrum of mental disorders, from preschoolers to the elderly. The popular press is replete with articles and information regarding the uses and abuses of psychiatric drugs, and pharmaceutical companies market their products directly to consumers in the form of full-page advertisements in popular magazines, as well as through radio and television commercials. Even prime time television news broadcasts have, from time to time, focused attention on the issue of psychiatric medication use and overuse in American society.

Pharmaceutical companies continue to develop psychiatric medications and support research efforts investigating new applications for existing drugs. The implications for practitioners regarding this flood of information, marketing, and associated medication use are important. Both the medical community and other nonmedical professionals (teachers, social workers, counselors, psychologists, etc.) are confronted daily with the ongoing challenge of remaining knowledgeable regarding the wide variety of psychotropic drugs now available. This challenge is complicated by the speed at which new drugs are introduced and

approved for use as well as by the medical and social issues surrounding their use. In this context, the term *psychotropic* refers to drug classes typically used in the treatment of psychiatric conditions such as ADHD, depression and other mood disorders, anxiety, and schizophrenia and other psychotic disorders. These medications include stimulants, antidepressants, antianxiety (anxiolytic) drugs, antipsychotic (neuroleptic) drugs, and some of the anticonvulsants.

The increasingly widespread use of psychopharmacology in the treatment of mental and behavioral disorders has important implications for both the medical profession and nonmedically trained human service professionals and educators. Today, teachers, counselors, social workers, and psychologists frequently work with individuals who take some type of psychiatric medication. It is essential for these professionals to have a basic understanding of the general classes of psychiatric medications, how they work, and their intended effects and side effects. This is important for several reasons. First, as already stated, the use of medications has become widespread. That in itself requires professionals to become more knowledgeable about psychotropic drugs. Second, teachers, counselors, and professionals in related fields are often front-line care providers and, as such, have ongoing, day-to-day contact with their students and clients. In this context, they are in a unique position to observe and monitor changes in behavior that may be due to the effects or side effects of medication. Third, the settings in which students and clients are seen are often well-controlled (e.g., classrooms, therapeutic treatment sites), allowing changes in behavior over time to be attributed more reliably to medication effects.

With these factors in mind, I have developed *Medication Fact Sheets* to provide educators and human service professionals with a handy and easy-to-understand reference to psychiatric medications. I believe psychologists, social workers, teachers, counselors, and others in the caring professions need a medication guide that addresses four basic medication questions.

What is it for?

What types of conditions or disorders are typically treated with a specific medication? Often, one medication may be prescribed for a variety of conditions. Conversely, a specific condition may respond to a variety of medications.

What does it do?

What biological, physical, cognitive, behavioral, and/or psychological effects does the medication produce?

What are the side effects?

What are common side effects I should watch for? Are there side effects that may be dangerous?

What are the dosages and forms?

How much is a large dose? For one medication, a large dose may be 2 milligrams per day. For another medication, it may be 2000 milligrams per day! What does the medication look like? In what forms is it available? How long before the medication takes effect?

The information included in this book was obtained primarily from pharmaceutical companies manufacturing and/or marketing specific medications, current FDA databases, and other reliable sources. Great care and effort was taken to insure that the information included in the Medication Fact Sheets is current and accurately represents the approved uses of each medication.

My intent is for *Medication Fact Sheets* to serve as a general overview of psychiatric medications. It is not meant as an exhaustive description of each medication, a prescribing guide, or a substitute for medical advice. Rather, it is intended as a quick, handy reference to address the four general questions posed above: What is it for? What does it do? What are the side effects? What are the dosages and forms? I trust you will find these pages useful in your professional practice.

References

Bradley, C. (1937). The behavior of children receiving benzedrine. *American Journal of Psychiatry, 94,* 577–585.

Ederheim, J. G. (2009). Off-label prescribing. *Psychiatric Times, 26*(4). Retrieved June 24, 2009, from www.psychiatrictimes.com/display/article/10168/1401983

A NOTE REGARDING "OFF-LABEL" USE OF MEDICATIONS

As part of the approval process, the Food and Drug Administration (FDA) requires that each medication be subjected to rigorous clinical trials to determine the drug's effectiveness for the condition or conditions it is designed to treat. Following successful clinical trials, the FDA approves and labels the medication for a particular condition or disease, identifies the recommended dosing, and indicates the specific population for which the drug has been tested and approved (e.g., adults 18 and older). It has long been common practice, however, for medications to be used in ways other than those specifically approved by the FDA. This is known as "off-label" use. It has been estimated that 40 to 60 percent of prescriptions are for off-label use (Ederheim, 2009). For example, it is not uncommon for medications that have been FDA-approved for adults to be used with children and adolescents, for drugs approved to treat schizophrenia also to be used to manage aggression or bipolar disorder, and so forth. The FDA has the primary role of regulating the manufacture, promotion, and labeling of medications, *not* regulating physicians. As you might expect, there has been substantial debate over the years as to the risks and benefits of off-label prescribing.

It is beyond the scope and purpose of this reference to address the wide array of off-label uses each medication may provide. Therefore, the information in each Medication Fact Sheet represents only the FDA-approved use for that specific medication.

What is it for?

Abilify is an atypical antipsychotic drug used in the treatment of schizophrenia in adults and adolescents over the age of 12. It has also been approved for treatment of manic and mixed episodes of Bipolar I disorder in adults and children as young as 10 and as an added treatment for major depression in adults.

What does it do?

Abilify has the effect of diminishing the symptoms of schizophrenia by reducing psychotic symptoms (delusions and hallucinations), in addition to improving cognitive functioning and mood. Pharmacologically, Abilify appears to block the central nervous system neurotransmitters dopamine and serotonin.

NOTE

Pregnancy Risk Category C (risk cannot be ruled out; see Appendix B).

What are the side effects?

Individuals taking Abilify may experience a wide range of side effects, including these:

1. Dizziness when standing up
2. Headache
3. Nausea/vomiting
4. Anxiety
5. Insomnia
6. Tardive dyskinesia/NMS

NOTES

► Tardive dyskinesia is a condition that may develop in individuals of any age group treated with antipsychotic medications for an extended period of time. Symptoms include involuntary movements of the face, tongue, mouth, or jaw and, to a lesser degree, involuntary rhythmic movements of the extremities. There is no known treatment for this condition.

► The medical literature has also reported the occurrence of neuroleptic malignant syndrome (NMS) in individuals taking antipsychotic medication. NMS is a rare but potentially fatal medication reaction involving a range of symptoms, including muscle rigidity, disorientation, irregular pulse and blood pressure, and tachycardia.

► Elderly individuals with dementia-related psychosis are at increased risk of death if treated with antipsychotic drugs and should not take Abilify.

► There is a risk of developing hyperglycemia and diabetes mellitus in individuals treated with atypical antipsychotic medications, including Abilify.

What are the dosages and forms?

The typical adult dosage range of Abilify for treatment of schizophrenia and Bipolar I mania is 10–30 mg/day administered in a single dose. As a supportive treatment for depression in adults, the dosage range is 5–15 mg/day. In adolescents with schizophrenia, the typical daily dosage range is 2–30 mg/day, and as a treatment for Bipolar I mania in children and adolescents, the dosage range is 2–30 mg/day. Abilify is well-absorbed and reaches peak plasma levels within 3–5 hours after administration. It may take up to 14 days for the full therapeutic effects of Abilify to become apparent.

► Tablet form (Bristol-Myers Squibb): 2 mg (rectangular, green); 5 mg (rectangular, blue); 10 mg (rectangular, pink); 15 mg (round, yellow); 20 mg (round, white); 30 mg (round, pink). Tablets are imprinted with the dosage strength. Abilify is also available as an orally disintegrating tablet (Abilify Discmelt): 10 mg (round, pink); 15 mg (round, yellow).

► Liquid form (Bristol-Myers Squibb): Abilify is available in liquid form (1.0 mg/mL).

► Injection form (Bristol-Myers Squibb): Ability is available as an intramuscular injection (9.75 mg/1.3mL).

This fact sheet is not intended to cover all possible medication uses, directions, precautions, drug interactions, or adverse effects and is not a substitute for specific medical advice or to be used as a guide for prescribing.

ADDERALL (Amphetamine/dextroamphetamine)

What is it for?

Adderall is a central nervous system stimulant that combines two stimulant drugs: amphetamine and dextroamphetamine. It is used in the treatment of attention-deficit/hyperactivity disorder (ADHD) in children and adults.

What does it do?

Stimulants have been shown to be useful in helping individuals improve behaviors commonly associated with ADHD, with effects such as these:

1. More controlled motor activity
2. Decreased disruptiveness
3. Improved concentration
4. Improved fine motor coordination
5. More goal-directed behavior
6. Decreased distractibility
7. Improved voice modulation

NOTE

Adderall is a controlled substance under DEA Schedule II (high potential for abuse; see Appendix C). Pregnancy Risk Category C (risk cannot be ruled out; see Appendix B).

What are the side effects?

Individuals taking Adderall may experience a wide range of side effects, including the following:

1. Nausea/upset stomach
2. Headache
3. Loss of appetite
4. Irritability
5. Dry mouth
6. Insomnia

NOTES

▸ Sudden death has been reported in individuals who have structural heart defects or other serious heart conditions.

▸ Medical literature reports that stimulants may intensify the motor and/or vocal tics characteristic of Tourette's syndrome.

▸ Individuals taking stimulant medications should not take monoamine oxidase inhibitors (MAOIs) at the same time or within 14 days of discontinuing treatment with an MAOI.

What are the dosages and forms?

As a treatment for ADHD, Adderall is not recommended for children under the age of 3. For children above the age of 6, dosages should not exceed 30 mg/day, given in divided doses throughout the day (usually at 4–6 hour intervals). Dosage is typically increased in 5 mg increments until the desired effect is obtained. Peak blood levels generally occur within 3 hours after ingestion. Adderall XR is given as a single daily dose in the morning, reaching peak blood levels in about 7 hours. The effective recommended daily dose for Adderall XR should not exceed 30 mg.

▸ Tablet form (various pharmaceutical companies): 5 mg; 7.5 mg; 10 mg; 12.5 mg; 15 mg; 20 mg; 30 mg. Tablets are round or ovoid. Colors may vary depending on manufacturer.

▸ Capsule form (Shire): Adderall XR (Extended Release), 5 mg (blue cap, clear body); 10 mg (blue cap, blue body); 15 mg (white cap, blue body); 20 mg (orange cap, orange body); 25 mg (white cap, orange body); 30 mg (orange cap, clear body).

From *Medication Fact Sheets: A Behavioral Medication Reference for Educators* (3rd ed.), © 2010 by D.E. Konopasek, Champaign IL: Research Press (800-519-2707, www.researchpress.com).

Oral Elavil is now available only as generic amitriptyline hydrochloride.

What is it for?

Amitriptyline is a tricyclic antidepressant used in the treatment of major depressive disorder (MDD).

What does it do?

Amitriptyline has the effect of elevating mood and improving cognitive and psychomotor functioning and concentration. Pharmacologically, it acts to block the reuptake of the central nervous system neurotransmitters norepinephrine and serotonin. Amitriptyline is one of the more sedating antidepressants.

NOTE

Pregnancy Risk Category C (risk cannot be ruled out; see Appendix B).

What are the side effects?

Individuals taking amitriptyline may experience a wide range of side effects, including the following:

1. Dry mouth
2. Tremors
3. Blurred vision
4. Constipation/urinary hesitance
5. Dizziness when standing up
6. Irregular heartbeat

NOTES

► It is recommended that amitriptyline not be taken in combination with monoamine oxidase inhibitors (MAOIs) or within 14 days of discontinuing treatment with an MAOI. At least 14 days should be allowed after stopping amitriptyline before starting an MAOI.

► Individuals taking amitriptyline should be monitored closely for the potential of worsening depression or the emergence of suicidal thoughts or behavior, particularly in the early stages of medication treatment or when dosages change.

What are the dosages and forms?

Amitriptyline is not recommended for children under the age of 12 due to a lack of research regarding its safety and effectiveness with this population. The typical adult dosage range is 75–150 mg/day, often given in divided doses. The therapeutic effect of amitriptyline may take up to 10 days to become apparent.

► Tablet form (Sandoz): 10 mg (round, pink); 25 mg (round, light green); 50 mg (round, brown); 75 mg (round, purple); 100 mg (round, orange).

Asendin is now available only as generic amoxapine.

What is it for?

Amoxapine is an atypical antidepressant and is used in the treatment of depression, particularly depression with associated psychotic symptoms, anxiety, or agitation.

What does it do?

Amoxapine has a mild sedative effect and is therefore sometimes selected for depressed individuals who are agitated or anxious. Pharmacologically, it appears to interfere with the reuptake of norepinephrine and serotonin as well as to block the effect of dopamine, all central nervous system neurotransmitters.

NOTE

Pregnancy Risk Category C (risk cannot be ruled out; see Appendix B).

What are the side effects?

Individuals taking amoxapine may experience a wide range of side effects, including the following:

1. Dry mouth
2. Nausea/constipation
3. Blurred vision
4. Restlessness/nervousness
5. Drowsiness/sedation
6. Tardive dyskinesia/NMS

NOTES

► Tardive dyskinesia is a condition that may develop in individuals of any age group treated with antipsychotic medications for an extended period of time. Symptoms include involuntary movements of the face, tongue, mouth, or jaw and, to a lesser degree, involuntary rhythmic movements of the extremities. There is no known treatment for this condition. Although amoxapine is not an antipsychotic medication, it has many properties common to neuroleptics.

► The medical literature has also reported the occurrence of neuroleptic malignant syndrome (NMS) in individuals taking antipsychotic medication. NMS is a rare but potentially fatal medication reaction involving a range of symptoms, including muscle rigidity, disorientation, irregular pulse and blood pressure, and tachycardia.

► It is recommended that amoxipine not be taken in combination with monoamine oxidase inhibitors (MAOIs) or within 14 days of discontinuing treatment with an MAOI. At least 14 days should be allowed after stopping amoxapine before starting an MAOI.

► Individuals taking amoxapine should be monitored closely for the potential of worsening depression or the emergence of suicidal thoughts or behavior, particularly in the early stages of medication treatment or when dosages change.

What are the dosages and forms?

The effectiveness and safety of amoxapine in children under the age of 16 has not been clinically determined. The usual adult dosage range is 200–300 mg/day, given either singly or in divided doses. Amoxapine is rapidly absorbed and reaches peak blood level in 2–4 hours. A therapeutic level of amoxapine may take up to 2 weeks to be observed.

► Tablet form (Watson): 25 mg (round, white); 50 mg (round, orange); 100 mg (round, blue); 150 mg (round, orange).

From *Medication Fact Sheets: A Behavioral Medication Reference for Educators* (3rd ed.), © 2010 by D.E. Konopasek, Champaign IL: Research Press (800-519-2707, www.researchpress.com).

Anafranil is available in generic form.

What is it for?

Although Anafranil is a tricyclic antidepressant, it is most often used in the treatment of obsessive-compulsive disorder (OCD).

What does it do?

Anafranil has the effect of reducing obsessive and compulsive behavior patterns and relieving associated symptoms of depression. Pharmacologically, Anafranil appears to block the reabsorption of serotonin, a central nervous system neurotransmitter.

NOTE

Pregnancy Risk Category C (risk cannot be ruled out; see Appendix B).

What are the side effects?

Individuals taking Anafranil may experience a wide range of side effects, including the following:

1. Upset stomach/nausea
2. Drowsiness/fatigue
3. Nervousness/tremors
4. Dizziness when standing up
5. Dry mouth/blurred vision
6. Difficulty urinating

NOTES

► The medical literature has reported the occurrence of seizures in individuals taking Anafranil.

► It is recommended that Anafranil not be taken in combination with monoamine oxidase inhibitors (MAOIs) or within 14 days of discontinuing treatment with an MAOI. At least 14 days should be allowed after stopping Anafranil before starting an MAOI.

► Individuals taking Anafranil should be monitored closely for the potential of worsening depression or the emergence of suicidal thoughts or behavior, particularly in the early stages of medication treatment or when dosages change.

What are the dosages and forms?

The safety and effectiveness of Anafranil in children under the age of 10 has not been established. The maximum dose for children and adolescents is 200 mg/day (or 3 mg/kg/day, whichever is smaller), typically given in divided doses initially to reduce stomach upset. For adults, the recommended maximum dose is 250 mg/day given as a single dose. Peak blood levels of Anafranil occur approximately 2–6 hours after ingestion, with effects lasting up to 36 hours. Initially, and as dosages change, it may take 2–3 weeks for the effects of Anafranil to reach a therapeutic level.

► Capsule form (Mallinckrodt): 25 mg (yellow cap, ivory body); 50 mg (blue cap, ivory body); 75 mg (yellow cap, ivory body). Capsules are imprinted with the word *ANAFRANIL* and the dosage.

This fact sheet is not intended to cover all possible medication uses, directions, precautions, drug interactions, or adverse effects and is not a substitute for specific medical advice or to be used as a guide for prescribing.

From *Medication Fact Sheets: A Behavioral Medication Reference for Educators* (3rd ed.), © 2010 by D.E. Konopasek, Champaign IL: Research Press (800-519-2707, www.researchpress.com).

Ativan is available in generic form.

What is it for?

Ativan is an antianxiety medication used in the short-term treatment of anxiety disorders and hypertension. It is used to help reduce anxiety associated with depression.

What does it do?

Ativan is a central nervous system depressant and has a tranquilizing effect on the central nervous system. Ativan belongs to the drug class benzodiazepine.

NOTE

Ativan is a controlled substance under DEA Schedule IV (see Appendix C). Pregnancy Risk Category D (positive evidence of risk; see Appendix B).

What are the side effects?

Individuals taking Ativan may experience a wide range of side effects, including the following:

1. Sedation
2. Dizziness
3. Nausea
4. Weakness
5. Unsteadiness
6. Change in appetite

NOTES

► Withdrawal symptoms (cramping, vomiting, convulsions, sweating, etc.) have been reported following abrupt discontinuation of Ativan. Individuals who are prone to substance abuse/addiction should be monitored carefully when taking Ativan due to the possibility for psychological and physiological dependence.

► Ativan is not recommended for individuals with narrow-angle glaucoma.

What are the dosages and forms?

The safety and effectiveness of Ativan in treating children under the age of 12 has not been clinically determined. The usual adult dose of Ativan may range from 2–6 mg/day given in divided doses. Ativan is fairly rapidly absorbed and reaches peak blood levels in about 2 hours, maintaining a therapeutic level for approximately 14 hours.

► Tablet form (Biovail): 0.5 mg (five-sided, white); 1 mg (five-sided, white); 2 mg (five-sided, white).

► Liquid form (Roxane): Lorazepam is available as an oral concentrate (2 mg/mL) as Lorazepam Intensol.

► Injection form (Baxter): Ativan is also available as an intramuscular injection (2 mg/mL).

This fact sheet is not intended to cover all possible medication uses, directions, precautions, drug interactions, or adverse effects and is not a substitute for specific medical advice or to be used as a guide for prescribing.

BENADRYL   (Diphenhydramine hydrochloride)

Benadryl is available in generic form.

What is it for?

Benadryl is an antihistamine medication. It is used to treat some allergic reactions to certain foods, as a treatment for motion sickness, and as a treatment for tremors and other "Parkinsonian" symptoms associated with the side effects of some antipsychotic medications.

What does it do?

Benadryl is an antihistamine with anticholinergic (drying) and sedative effects.

NOTE

Pregnancy Risk Category B (no evidence of risk in humans; see Appendix B).

What are the side effects?

Individuals taking Benadryl may experience a wide range of side effects, including the following:

1. Gastric distress
2. Perspiration
3. Dry mouth
4. Sedation
5. Dizziness
6. Impaired coordination

What are the dosages and forms?

The usual adult dosage of Benadryl is 75–200 mg/day, given in divided doses. In children, the dosage may range from 50–100 mg/day. The daily dosage for children should not exceed 300 mg. Benadryl is fairly rapidly absorbed into the bloodstream and maintains a therapeutic level for 4–6 hours.

- Forms of administration (various pharmaceutical companies): Benadryl is available in many forms, including capsule, tablet, syrup, elixir, creams, chewable tablets, injection, and sprays.

This fact sheet is not intended to cover all possible medication uses, directions, precautions, drug interactions, or adverse effects and is not a substitute for specific medical advice or to be used as a guide for prescribing.

From *Medication Fact Sheets: A Behavioral Medication Reference for Educators* (3rd ed.), © 2010 by D.E. Konopasek, Champaign IL: Research Press (800-519-2707, www.researchpress.com).

BuSPAR (Buspirone hydrochloride)

BuSpar is available in generic form.

What is it for?

BuSpar is an antianxiety drug and is often used to treat generalized anxiety disorder (GAD). It is also used occasionally to treat individuals who may become aggressive. BuSpar is sometimes preferred for the elderly and addiction-prone individuals due to its nonsedating effects and lower potential for abuse compared with other antianxiety medications.

What does it do?

The chemical mechanism of BuSpar's action is unknown, although it is thought to influence concentrations of dopamine and serotonin, both central nervous system neurotransmitters. It has the effect of calming and reducing anxiety.

NOTE

Pregnancy Risk Category B (no evidence of risk in humans; see Appendix B).

What are the side effects?

Individuals taking BuSpar may experience a wide range of side effects, including the following:

1. Headache
2. Dizziness
3. Insomnia
4. Nausea
5. Nervousness/lightheadedness
6. Drowsiness

NOTES

► It is recommended that BuSpar not be taken in combination with monoamine oxidase inhibitors (MAOIs) or within 14 days of discontinuing treatment with an MAOI. At least 14 days should be allowed after stopping BuSpar before starting an MAOI.

► Drinking large amounts of grapefruit juice while taking BuSpar is not recommended.

What are the dosages and forms?

The usefulness or safety of BuSpar in children under the age of 6 has not been clinically determined. The adult dosage range for BuSpar is 15–60 mg/day, usually given in 2–3 divided doses. Peak blood levels occur within approximately 40–90 minutes.

► Tablet form (Bristol-Myers Squibb): 5 mg (ovoid-rectangular, white); 10 mg (ovoid-rectangular, white); 15 mg (rectangular, white); 30 mg (rectangular, pink). The 5 and 10 mg tablets are imprinted with the dosage strength and the word *BuSpar*. The 15 mg DIVIDOSE tablet is imprinted with the letters *MJ* and the number *822* and is scored so that it can be either bisected or trisected. The 30 mg DIVIDOSE tablet has the number *824* on one side and, on the other side, the number *10* on each of the scored trisections.

This fact sheet is not intended to cover all possible medication uses, directions, precautions, drug interactions, or adverse effects and is not a substitute for specific medical advice or to be used as a guide for prescribing.

From *Medication Fact Sheets: A Behavioral Medication Reference for Educators* (3rd ed.), © 2010 by D.E. Konopasek, Champaign IL: Research Press (800-519-2707, www.researchpress.com).

Catapres is available in generic form.

What is it for?

Catapres is frequently used in the treatment of anxiety and hypertension. It has also been used to help decrease distressing physiological symptoms associated with opioid withdrawal (e.g., palpitations, sweating). It has been used to treat attention-deficit/hyperactivity disorder (ADHD) as well as to suppress tics associated with Tourette's syndrome.

What does it do?

Catapres is an antihypertensive medication that exerts a calming effect by reducing blood pressure, pulse rate, and central nervous system stimulation.

NOTE

Pregnancy Risk Category C (risk cannot be ruled out; see Appendix B).

What are the side effects?

Individuals taking Catapres may experience a wide range of side effects, including the following:

1. Dry mouth
2. Sedation
3. Hypotension (low blood pressure)
4. Dizziness
5. Constipation
6. Nausea/vomiting

NOTE

Individuals should not stop taking Catapres without consulting their physician. Stopping Catapres suddenly may cause nervousness, tremors, headache, and/or elevated blood pressure. Instead, a gradual discontinuation is recommended.

What are the dosages and forms?

The safety of Catapres for use in children under the age of 12 has not yet been determined. The adult dosage range for Catapres is 0.2–0.6 mg/day, given in divided doses. Catapres acts fairly rapidly. Blood pressure declines within 30–60 minutes after ingestion, with peak blood levels occurring within about 3–5 hours and remaining at a therapeutic blood level for 12–16 hours.

► Tablet form (Boehringer Ingelheim): 0.1 mg (oval, tan) imprinted *BI 6;* 0.2 mg (oval, orange) imprinted *BI 7;* 0.3 mg (oval, peach) imprinted *BI 11.*

► Transdermal therapeutic system (TTS) (Boehringer Ingelheim): Catapres is available as a transdermal patch in the same dosages as the tablet form. Patches are labeled *Catapres-TTS-1, TTS-2,* and *TTS-3,* corresponding to dosages of 0.1 mg, 0.2 mg, and 0.3 mg, respectively. Patches should be reapplied every 7 days.

This fact sheet is not intended to cover all possible medication uses, directions, precautions, drug interactions, or adverse effects and is not a substitute for specific medical advice or to be used as a guide for prescribing.

CELEXA   (Citalopram hydrobromide)

Celexa is available in generic form.

What is it for?

Celexa is an antidepressant and is used in the treatment of major depressive disorder (MDD).

What does it do?

Celexa belongs to a group of antidepressants known as selective serotonin reuptake inhibitors (SSRIs). As such, it acts to block, or inhibit, the reabsorption of serotonin, a central nervous system neurotransmitter. The intended effect is elevation of mood, improved cognitive and psychomotor functioning, and improved concentration.

NOTE

Pregnancy Risk Category C (risk cannot be ruled out; see Appendix B).

What are the side effects?

Individuals taking Celexa may experience a wide range of side effects, including the following:

1. Nausea/vomiting
2. Dry mouth
3. Sleepiness or insomnia
4. Irregular heartbeat
5. Dizziness when standing up
6. Increased sweating

NOTES

► It is recommended that Celexa not be taken in combination with monoamine oxidase inhibitors (MAOIs) or within 14 days of discontinuing treatment with an MAOI. At least 14 days should be allowed after stopping Celexa before starting an MAOI.

► Individuals taking Celexa should be monitored closely for the potential of worsening depression or the emergence of suicidal thoughts or behavior, particularly in the early stages of medication treatment or when dosages change.

► A serious, potentially life-threatening condition known as serotonin syndrome can occur when SSRIs and certain medications used to treat migraine headaches (triptans) are taken together.

What are the dosages and forms?

The usefulness and safety of Celexa in children has not been established. The adult dosage range for Celexa is 20–40 mg/day, usually given in a single dose either in the morning or evening. Peak blood levels occur approximately 4 hours after ingestion. It may take a week for the full therapeutic effect of Celexa to become apparent.

► Tablet form (Forest): 10 mg (oval, beige); 20 mg (oval, pink); 40 mg (oval, white). Each tablet is imprinted with the letters *F* and *P*, along with the dosage.

► Liquid form (Forest): Celexa is available in liquid form as a solution (10 mg/5 mL).

This fact sheet is not intended to cover all possible medication uses, directions, precautions, drug interactions, or adverse effects and is not a substitute for specific medical advice or to be used as a guide for prescribing.

From *Medication Fact Sheets: A Behavioral Medication Reference for Educators* (3rd ed.), © 2010 by D.E. Konopasek, Champaign IL: Research Press (800-519-2707, www.researchpress.com).

What is it for?

Celontin is an anticonvulsant and is used in the treatment of absence (petit mal) seizures.

What does it do?

Celontin reduces seizure activity by suppressing abnormal brain action. It depresses the motor cortex and elevates the seizure threshold.

NOTE

Pregnancy Risk Category C (risk cannot be ruled out; see Appendix B).

What are the side effects?

Individuals taking Celontin may experience a wide range of side effects, including the following:

1. Loss of appetite
2. Nausea/vomiting
3. Weight loss
4. Headache
5. Dizziness
6. Drowsiness

NOTES

► The medical literature reports the occurrence of potentially life-threatening blood disorders associated with Celontin. Therefore, it is recommended that patients taking Celontin have periodic blood counts.

► Antiseizure drugs should not be discontinued abruptly due to a risk of increased seizure activity.

What are the dosages and forms?

The recommended starting dose for adults is 300 mg/day. After a week, the dosage may be increased in 300 mg increments to achieve a maximum therapeutic dose of 1.2 grams/day. The smaller 150-mg tablet is often easier for children to ingest. Celontin may be administered with other anticonvulsant medications if other types of seizure disorders coexist with absence seizures.

► Capsule form (Parke-Davis/Pfizer): 150 mg (white body, yellow cap); 300 mg (white body, yellow cap).

This fact sheet is not intended to cover all possible medication uses, directions, precautions, drug interactions, or adverse effects and is not a substitute for specific medical advice or to be used as a guide for prescribing.

From *Medication Fact Sheets: A Behavioral Medication Reference for Educators* (3rd ed.), © 2010 by D.E. Konopasek, Champaign IL: Research Press (800-519-2707, www.researchpress.com).

Thorazine is now available only as generic chlorpromazine.

What is it for?

Chlorpromazine has been used in the management of psychotic disorders. It is occasionally used to manage severe behavior problems in children, such as combativeness or explosive excitability. It has also been used to control severe hiccups, relieve presurgical anxiety, and control nausea and vomiting.

What does it do?

Pharmacologically, chlorpromazine seems to act by blocking the action of dopamine, a central nervous system neurotransmitter. It is sedating and helps to reduce psychotic symptoms or calm individuals who are combative or hyperexcited.

NOTE

Pregnancy Risk Category C (risk cannot be ruled out; see Appendix B).

What are the side effects?

Individuals taking chlorpromazine may experience a wide range of side effects, including the following:

1. Sedation/fatigue
2. Agitation/restlessness
3. Tremors/shakiness
4. Hypotension/dizziness
5. Dry mouth/blurred vision
6. Tardive dyskinesia/NMS

NOTES

► Tardive dyskinesia is a condition that may develop in individuals of any age group treated with antipsychotic medications for an extended period of time. Symptoms include involuntary movements of the face, tongue, mouth, or jaw and, to a lesser degree, involuntary rhythmic movements of the extremities. There is no known treatment for this condition.

► The medical literature has also reported the occurrence of neuroleptic malignant syndrome (NMS) in individuals taking antipsychotic medication. NMS is a rare but potentially fatal medication reaction involving a range of symptoms, including muscle rigidity, disorientation, irregular pulse and blood pressure, and tachycardia.

► Chlorpromazine should not be used in children or adolescents showing any symptoms of Reye's syndrome.

What are the dosages and forms?

To manage behavior problems in children, the recommended dose is 0.25 mg/lb every 4–6 hours (e.g., a child weighing 60 pounds would receive a dose of 15 mg every 4–6 hours). The daily dose for adults ranges from 200–800 mg, given in divided doses. Generally, doses above 1000 mg/day are not recommended. Maximum improvement in the treatment of psychotic symptoms may not become apparent for weeks.

► Tablet form (Sandoz): 10 mg (round, orange); 25 mg (round, orange); 50 mg (round, orange); 100 mg (round, orange); 200 mg (round, orange).

► Other forms (various pharmaceutical companies): Chlorpromazine is also available in ampules, syrup, concentrate, suppositories, and intramuscular injection.

This fact sheet is not intended to cover all possible medication uses, directions, precautions, drug interactions, or adverse effects and is not a substitute for specific medical advice or to be used as a guide for prescribing.

From *Medication Fact Sheets: A Behavioral Medication Reference for Educators* (3rd ed.), © 2010 by D.E. Konopasek, Champaign IL: Research Press (800-519-2707, www.researchpress.com).

Clozaril is available in generic form.

What is it for?

Clozaril is an atypical antipsychotic drug and is used in the management of individuals with treatment resistant schizophrenia, especially those who exhibit patterns of suicidal behavior.

What does it do?

Clozaril appears to block the action of the neurotransmitter dopamine by binding with dopamine receptor sites. It has the effect of decreasing psychotic symptoms and agitation and increasing cognitive functioning.

NOTE

Pregnancy Risk Category B (no evidence of risk in humans; see Appendix B).

What are the side effects?

Individuals taking Clozaril may experience a wide range of side effects, including the following:

1. Sedation/drowsiness
2. Tachycardia/Myocarditis
3. Seizures
4. Dizziness when standing up
5. Gastrointestinal distress
6. Agranulocytosis
7. Tardive dyskinesia/NMS

NOTES

- There is an increased risk of cardiac inflammation or degeneration associated with Clozaril.

- There is a significant risk of seizures associated with taking Clozaril, with higher risk associated with higher dosage.

- Agranulocytosis is a rare but serious blood disorder whereby the white blood cell count drops precipitously, causing a serious risk of death because of lowered resistance to infection. Due to the risk of agranulocytosis, Clozaril is available only through a distribution system requiring regular blood testing.

- Tardive dyskinesia is a condition that may develop in individuals of any age group treated with antipsychotic medications for an extended period of time. Symptoms include involuntary movements of the face, tongue, mouth, or jaw and, to a lesser degree, involuntary rhythmic movements of the extremities. There is no known treatment for this condition.

- Neuroleptic malignant syndrome (NMS) has been associated with the use of antipsychotic medications. NMS is a rare but potentially fatal medication reaction involving a range of symptoms, including muscle rigidity, disorientation, irregular pulse and blood pressure, and tachycardia.

- There is an increased risk of death in elderly individuals with dementia-related psychosis who are being treated with Clozaril.

- There is a risk of developing hyperglycemia and diabetes mellitus in individuals treated with atypical antipsychotic medications, including Clozaril.

What are the dosages and forms?

The safety and effectiveness of Clozaril for children has not yet been determined. For adults, the initial dose is typically 12.5–25 mg given once or twice daily. Many adults tolerate daily doses ranging from 300–450 mg, given in three doses. Dosage should not exceed 900 mg/day.

- Tablet form (Novartis): 25 mg (round, pale yellow); 100 mg (round, pale yellow). Tablets have the word *CLOZARIL* engraved on one side and the dosage strength engraved on the other. Generic clozapine is also available as a 12.5 mg tablet (Ivax Pharmaceuticals).

- Orally disintegrating form (Azur Pharma): Clozapine is available in an orally disintegrating form as Fazaclo in 12.5 mg (round, yellow); 25 mg (round, yellow); 100 mg (round, yellow).

Oral Cogentin is now available only as generic benztropine mesylate.

What is it for?

Cogentin is used in the treatment of tremors associated with Parkinson's disease as well as for tremors and shakiness (extrapyramidal symptoms) associated with the side effects of some antipsychotic medications.

What does it do?

Cogentin is an anticholinergic medication that inhibits the action of acetylcholine, a central nervous system neurotransmitter, exerting a relaxing effect on the muscles.

NOTE

Pregnancy Risk Category C (risk cannot be ruled out; see Appendix B).

What are the side effects?

Individuals taking Cogentin may experience a wide range of side effects, including the following:

1. Constipation
2. Difficulty urinating
3. Headache
4. Blurred vision/dry mouth
5. Irregular heartbeat
6. Nausea/vomiting

What are the dosages and forms?

Cogentin is not recommended for children under the age of 3 and should be used with caution in older children. The usual adult dosage range of Cogentin is 1–4 mg once or twice per day as needed to relieve Parkinsonian symptoms caused by antipsychotic medications. After 1–2 weeks, Cogentin is often discontinued to determine whether Parkinsonian symptoms will return. If they do, Cogentin may be reinstated.

► Tablet form (Merck): 0.5 mg (round, white); 1 mg (oval, white); 2 mg (round, white).

► Injection form (Ovation): Cogentin may be administered as an intramuscular injection (1 mg/mL).

This fact sheet is not intended to cover all possible medication uses, directions, precautions, drug interactions, or adverse effects and is not a substitute for specific medical advice or to be used as a guide for prescribing.

From *Medication Fact Sheets: A Behavioral Medication Reference for Educators* (3rd ed.), © 2010 by D.E. Konopasek, Champaign IL: Research Press (800-519-2707, www.researchpress.com).

What is it for?

Concerta is most often used as a treatment for attention-deficit/hyperactivity disorder (ADHD) in children 6 years of age and older and in adults up to age 65.

What does it do?

Concerta is a central nervous system stimulant. It appears to block the reuptake of norepinephrine and dopamine, both central nervous system neurotransmitters. Stimulants have been shown to be useful in helping individuals improve behaviors commonly associated with ADHD, with effects such as these:

1. Improved motor activity
2. Decreased disruptiveness
3. Improved concentration
4. Improved fine motor coordination
5. More goal-directed behavior
6. Decreased distractibility
7. Improved voice modulation

NOTE

Concerta is a controlled substance under DEA Schedule II (high potential for abuse; see Appendix C). Pregnancy Risk Category C (risk cannot be ruled out; see Appendix B).

What are the side effects?

Individuals taking Concerta may experience a wide range of side effects, including the following:

1. Loss of appetite
2. Insomnia
3. Stomachache
4. Irritability and anxiety
5. Headache
6. Dizziness

NOTES

► Sudden death has been reported in individuals taking stimulant medications who have structural heart defects or other serious heart conditions.

► Medical literature reports that stimulants may intensify the motor and/or vocal tics characteristic of Tourette's syndrome.

► Concerta should not be used in individuals with glaucoma.

► Individuals taking stimulant medications should not take monoamine oxidase inhibitors (MAOIs) at the same time or within 14 days of discontinuing treatment with an MAOI.

What are the dosages and forms?

Concerta has not been studied in children under the age of 6. In children over the age of 6, the dosage should not exceed 54 mg/day. The typical adolescent/adult dosage range is 18–72 mg/day, given in a single morning dose. In adults, the initial therapeutic effect of a single dose of Concerta occurs within approximately 1–2 hours, then gradually increases and reaches peak levels in 6–10 hours, after which the effect gradually weakens. Concerta is available only in extended-release tablet form.

► Tablet form (Alza): 18 mg (capsule-shaped, yellow); 27 mg (capsule-shaped, gray); 36 mg (capsule-shaped, white); 54 mg (capsule-shaped, brownish red). Tablets are imprinted with *alza* along with the dosage strength.

What is it for?

Cymbalta is an antidepressant approved for the treatment of major depressive disorder (MDD). It is also used in the treatment of generalized anxiety disorder (GAD), as well as pain associated with diabetic peripheral neuropathy and fibromyalgia.

What does it do?

Cymbalta is a selective serotonin and norepinephrine reuptake inhibitor (SSNRI). It appears to increase the availability and activity of the neurotransmitters serotonin and norepinephrine. The intended effect is an elevation of mood, improved cognitive and psychomotor functioning, and improved concentration.

NOTE

Pregnancy Risk Category C (risk cannot be ruled out; see Appendix B).

What are the side effects?

Individuals taking Cymbalta may experience a wide range of side effects, including the following:

1. Nausea
2. Dry mouth
3. Constipation
4. Decreased appetite
5. Fatigue/sleepiness
6. Increased sweating

NOTES

► It is recommended that Cymbalta not be taken in combination with monoamine oxidase inhibitors (MAOIs) or within 14 days of discontinuing treatment with an MAOI. At least 14 days should be allowed after stopping Cymbalta before starting an MAOI.

► Individuals taking Cymbalta should be monitored closely for the potential of worsening depression or the emergence of suicidal thoughts or behavior, particularly in the early stages of medication treatment or when dosages change.

► Cymbalta should not be taken by individuals with narrow angle glaucoma.

► Cases of liver failure have been reported in individuals taking Cymbalta.

► A serious, potentially life-threatening condition known as serotonin syndrome can occur when SSRIs and certain medications used to treat migraine headaches (triptans) are taken together.

What are the dosages and forms?

The safety of Cymbalta in children and adolescents under the age of 18 has not been clinically established. The typical adult dosage range of Cymbalta as a treatment for depression or GAD is 40–60 mg/day administered in a single or divided dose. Cymbalta is well absorbed and reaches peak plasma levels in approximately 6–10 hours after administration. Steady state concentrations typically occur after 3 days of treatment.

► Capsule form (Eli Lilly): 20 mg (green body, green cap); 30 mg (white body, blue cap); 60 mg (green body, blue cap). Cymbalta is available only in delayed release form. Capsules are imprinted with *LILLY* on the cap and the dosage strength on the body.

This fact sheet is not intended to cover all possible medication uses, directions, precautions, drug interactions, or adverse effects and is not a substitute for specific medical advice or to be used as a guide for prescribing.

DALMANE   (Flurazepam hydrochloride)

Dalmane is available in generic form.

What is it for?

Dalmane is used as a short-term treatment for insomnia (i.e., difficulty falling asleep, frequent awakenings, or early awakenings).

What does it do?

Dalmane is a central nervous system depressant and helps induce sleep by blocking the arousal of certain higher functioning brain centers. Dalmane belongs to the drug class benzodiazepine.

NOTE

Dalmane is a controlled substance under DEA Schedule IV (see Appendix C). Pregnancy Risk Category X (contraindicated in pregnancy; see Appendix B).

What are the side effects?

Individuals taking Dalmane may experience a wide range of side effects, including the following:

1. Dizziness
2. Drowsiness
3. Depression
4. Disorientation
5. Upset stomach
6. Impaired coordination

NOTE

Withdrawal symptoms, (cramping, vomiting, convulsions, sweating, etc.) have been reported following abrupt discontinuation of Dalmane. Individuals who are prone to substance abuse/addiction should be monitored carefully when taking Dalmane due to the possibility for psychological and physiological dependence.

What are the dosages and forms?

The use of Dalmane in children under the age of 15 is not recommended due to the lack of clinical studies demonstrating its usefulness with that age group. The usual dosage range for adults is 15–30 mg/day, given at bedtime. Dalmane enters the bloodstream very quickly, with peak blood levels occurring within 30–60 minutes after ingestion.

► Capsule form (Valeant): 15 mg (orange cap, ivory body); 30 mg (red cap, ivory body).

This fact sheet is not intended to cover all possible medication uses, directions, precautions, drug interactions, or adverse effects and is not a substitute for specific medical advice or to be used as a guide for prescribing.

Methylphenidate is available in generic form, although not as a transdermal patch.

What is it for?

Daytrana is most often used as a treatment for attention-deficit/hyperactivity disorder (ADHD).

What does it do?

Daytrana appears to block the reuptake of norepinephrine and dopamine, both central nervous system neurotransmitters. Stimulants have been shown to be useful in helping individuals improve behaviors commonly associated with ADHD, with effects such as these:

1. Improved motor activity
2. Decreased disruptiveness
3. Improved concentration
4. Improved fine motor coordination
5. More goal-directed behavior
6. Decreased distractibility
7. Improved voice modulation

NOTE

Daytrana is a controlled substance under DEA Schedule II (high potential for abuse; see Appendix C). Pregnancy Risk Category C (risk cannot be ruled out; see Appendix B).

What are the side effects?

Individuals taking Daytrana may experience a wide range of side effects, including the following:

1. Loss of appetite
2. Insomnia
3. Upset stomach
4. Irritability and anxiety
5. Headache
6. Dizziness

NOTES

► Sudden death has been reported in individuals taking stimulant medications who have structural heart defects or other serious heart conditions.

► Medical literature reports that stimulants may intensify the motor and/or vocal tics characteristic of Tourette's syndrome.

► Daytrana should not be used in individuals with glaucoma.

► Individuals taking stimulant medications should not take monoamine oxidase inhibitors (MAOIs) at the same time or within 14 days of discontinuing treatment with an MAOI.

What are the dosages and forms?

Daytrana has not been studied in children under the age of 6. Daytrana delivers a metered dose of methylphenidate over an approximately 9-hour period via an adhesive transdermal patch attached to the hip.

► Transdermal Patch System (Shire): Dosage equivalents are based upon patch size, as follows: The 12.5 square cm patch, 18.75 square cm patch, 25 square cm patch, and 37.5 square cm patch contain 27.5 mg, 41.3 mg, 55 mg, and 82.5 mg of methylphenidate, respectively.

From *Medication Fact Sheets: A Behavioral Medication Reference for Educators* (3rd ed.), © 2010 by D.E. Konopasek, Champaign IL: Research Press (800-519-2707, www.researchpress.com).

Depakene is available in generic form. DEPAKOTE, DEPAKOTE SPRINKLES, and DEPAKOTE ER are trade names for divalproex sodium. DEPACON is the trade name for valproate sodium.

What is it for?

Depakene is an anticonvulsant medication used in the treatment of simple and complex absence (petit mal) seizures and partial-complex seizures. Depakote has also been used to treat the manic phase of bipolar disorder. Both Depakote and Depakote ER have been used as a preventative treatment for migraine headaches.

What does it do?

Depakene is effective in reducing seizure activity. Pharmacologically, it appears to suppress the spread of abnormal or diffuse electrical discharges in the brain that cause seizures.

NOTE

Pregnancy Risk Category D (positive evidence of risk; see Appendix B).

What are the side effects?

Individuals taking Depakene may experience a wide range of side effects, including the following:

1. Sedation/headache
2. Tremors
3. Weight gain
4. Nausea/vomiting
5. Poor coordination/weakness
6. Liver/pancreatic toxicity

NOTES

- There is a risk of severe, sometimes fatal liver toxicity associated with Depakene, Depakote Sprinkles, Depakote ER, and Depacon. The vast majority of fatalities have occurred in children under the age of 2. Particularly at risk are those children taking multiple anticonvulsants. Monitoring liver function is important. In addition, potentially life-threatening pancreatitis in both children and adults has been associated with Depakene.

- There is a risk of birth defects, such as spina bifida, if Depakene or its derivatives are taken during pregnancy.

- Antiseizure drugs should not be discontinued abruptly due to a risk of increased seizure activity.

What are the dosages and forms?

For adults and children over the age of 10, the maximum recommended dosage of Depakene is 60 mg/kg/day. Depakene is rapidly absorbed after ingestion, with peak blood levels occurring 1–4 hours later. The blood level half-life is 6–16 hours.

- Delayed/Sustained release tablet form (Abbott): DEPAKOTE 125 mg (oval, salmon pink); 250 mg (oval, peach); 500 mg (oval, lavender). DEPACOTE ER: 250 mg (oval, white); 500 mg (oval, gray).

- Capsule form (Abbott): 250 mg (orange cap, orange body) imprinted with *DEPAKENE*. Also available as DEPAKOTE SPRINKLES 125 mg (blue cap, white body).

- Liquid form (Abbott): Depakene is available in syrup form (250 mg/5 mL).

- Intravenous form (Abbott): DEPACON is available as an intravenous infusion.

This fact sheet is not intended to cover all possible medication uses, directions, precautions, drug interactions, or adverse effects and is not a substitute for specific medical advice or to be used as a guide for prescribing.

What is it for?

Desoxyn is used for short-term treatment of obesity in individuals who have not responded to alternative treatments. It has also infrequently been used in the treatment of attention-deficit/hyperactivity disorder (ADHD).

What does it do?

Desoxyn is a central nervous system stimulant. Stimulants can be useful in helping individuals improve behaviors common to ADHD, with effects such as these:

1. Improved motor activity
2. Decreased disruptiveness
3. Improved concentration
4. Improved fine motor coordination
5. More goal-directed behavior
6. Decreased distractibility
7. Improved voice modulation

NOTE

Desoxyn is a controlled substance under DEA Schedule II (high potential for abuse; see Appendix C). Pregnancy Risk Category C (risk cannot be ruled out; see Appendix B).

What are the side effects?

Individuals taking Desoxyn may experience a wide range of side effects, including the following:

1. Insomnia/overstimulation
2. Rapid heartbeat
3. Elevated blood pressure
4. Dizziness
5. Upset stomach/diarrhea
6. Headache

NOTES

► Sudden death has been reported in individuals taking stimulant medications who have structural heart defects or other serious heart conditions.

► Medical literature reports that stimulants may intensify the motor and/or vocal tics characteristic of Tourette's syndrome.

► Individuals taking stimulant medications should not take monoamine oxidase inhibitors (MAOIs) at the same time or within 14 days of discontinuing treatment with an MAOI.

What are the dosages and forms?

The safety of Desoxyn in children under the age of 12 has not been established. As part of the treatment for ADHD in children 6 years and older, the usual daily dose is 20–25 mg, given either once or divided into two doses. Desoxyn is rapidly absorbed into the bloodstream, with a half-life of 4–5 hours.

► Tablet form (Ovation): 5 mg (round, white).

This fact sheet is not intended to cover all possible medication uses, directions, precautions, drug interactions, or adverse effects and is not a substitute for specific medical advice or to be used as a guide for prescribing.

From *Medication Fact Sheets: A Behavioral Medication Reference for Educators* (3rd ed.), © 2010 by D.E. Konopasek, Champaign IL: Research Press (800-519-2707, www.researchpress.com).

Dexedrine is available in generic form.

What is it for?

Dexedrine is used in the treatment of attention-deficit/hyperactivity disorder (ADHD). In adults, Dexedrine is also occasionally used in the treatment of obesity and narcolepsy (sudden, usually brief attacks of deep sleep).

What does it do?

Dexedrine is a central nervous system stimulant. It has been shown to be useful in helping individuals improve behaviors commonly associated with ADHD, with effects such as these:

1. Improved motor activity
2. Decreased disruptiveness
3. Improved fine motor skills
4. More goal-directed behavior
5. Decreased distractibility

NOTE

Dexedrine is a controlled substance under DEA Schedule II (high potential for abuse; see Appendix C). Pregnancy Risk Category C (risk cannot be ruled out; see Appendix B).

What are the side effects?

Individuals taking Dexedrine may experience a wide range of side effects, including the following:

1. Loss of appetite
2. Insomnia
3. Restlessness/dizziness
4. Irritability and anxiety
5. Dry mouth
6. Palpitations/tachycardia

NOTES

- Sudden death has been reported in individuals taking stimulant medications who have structural heart defects or other serious heart conditions.

- Medical literature reports that stimulants may intensify the motor and/or vocal tics characteristic of Tourette's syndrome.

- Individuals taking stimulant medications should not take monoamine oxidase inhibitors (MAOIs) at the same time or within 14 days of discontinuing treatment with an MAOI.

What are the dosages and forms?

For treating ADHD in children 3 years old and older, the typical dose ranges from 5–40 mg/day. Dosage is usually increased weekly in 5-mg increments until the desired response is obtained. Peak blood effects generally occur about 3 hours after ingestion. Tablet doses are typically given initially upon awakening, then at 4–6 hour intervals. Spansules are usually given as a single dose in the morning.

- Tablet Form (various pharmaceutical companies), 5 mg. Dextrostat (Shire), 5 mg (round, yellow); 10 mg (round, yellow).

- Sustained release capsule (Spansule) form (GlaxoSmithKline): 5, 10, or 15 mg (brown cap, clear body). Peak blood effects generally occur about 8 hours after ingestion.

- Oral solution form (Outlook): 5 mg/mL

This fact sheet is not intended to cover all possible medication uses, directions, precautions, drug interactions, or adverse effects and is not a substitute for specific medical advice or to be used as a guide for prescribing.

From *Medication Fact Sheets: A Behavioral Medication Reference for Educators* (3rd ed.), © 2010 by D.E. Konopasek, Champaign IL: Research Press (800-519-2707, www.researchpress.com).

Dilantin is available in generic form.

What is it for?

Dilantin is an anticonvulsant useful in the treatment of tonic-clonic, grand mal, and temporal lobe seizure disorders. It has also been used as a seizure preventative during neurosurgery. Dilantin does not seem to be as effective in the treatment of absence (petit mal) seizures.

What does it do?

Dilantin appears to act primarily on the motor cortex area of the brain, where it inhibits the spread of seizure activity. This effect controls the spread of electrical impulses along nerve pathways, reducing or eliminating the occurrence of seizures.

NOTE

Pregnancy Risk Category D (positive evidence of risk; see Appendix B).

What are the side effects?

Individuals taking Dilantin may experience a wide range of side effects, including the following:

1. Rapid eye movement
2. Nausea/vomiting
3. Insomnia
4. Slurred speech
5. Tender or swollen gums
6. Nervousness/twitching

NOTES

- Antiseizure drugs should not be discontinued abruptly due to a risk of increased seizure activity.
- Dilantin is also available in combination with Phenobarbitol.

What are the dosages and forms?

The usual dose for children is 5 mg/kg/day, to a maximum of 300 mg/day, generally given in two or three divided doses. Children above age 6 and adolescents may need the minimum adult dose of 300 mg/day. The usual adult dosage is approximately 300–400 mg/day to a maximum of 600 mg/day, given in divided doses. Dilantin Kapseals usually reach peak blood levels within 4–12 hours after ingestion, with a full steady state therapeutic level generally reached in 7 to 10 days.

- Chewable tablet form (Pfizer): Infatabs (not for once a day dosing): 50 mg (triangular, white).

- Extended release capsule form (Pfizer): Kapseals 30 mg (white with pink band); 100 mg (white with red band). An alternate capsule form (Pfizer): 100 mg (medium orange cap, opaque body). Additional strengths of extended release phenytoin (200 mg, 300 mg) are available as Phenytek (Mylan).

- Injection form (various pharmaceutical companies): Phenytoin is available as an intramuscular injection (50 mg/mL) both generically and under the brand name Cerebyx (Pfizer).

- Liquid form (various pharmaceutical companies): Dilantin is available as a liquid suspension for children (125 mg/5 mL).

This fact sheet is not intended to cover all possible medication uses, directions, precautions, drug interactions, or adverse effects and is not a substitute for specific medical advice or to be used as a guide for prescribing.

From *Medication Fact Sheets: A Behavioral Medication Reference for Educators* (3rd ed.), © 2010 by D.E. Konopasek, Champaign IL: Research Press (800-519-2707, www.researchpress.com).

DIOVAN   (Valsartan)

What is it for?

Diovan is used in the treatment of hypertension. It may be used alone or in combination with other hypertension medications. It is also used as a treatment for heart failure.

What does it do?

Diovan acts to lower blood pressure and stabilize heart rate by reducing the constriction of blood vessels.

NOTE

Pregnancy Risk Category D (Positive evidence of risk; see Appendix B).

What are the side effects?

Individuals taking Diovan may experience a wide range of side effects, including these:

1. Headache/dizziness
2. Fatigue
3. Diarrhea
4. Flu-like symptoms
5. Abdominal pain
6. Nausea

What are the dosages and forms?

Diovan enters the system fairly rapidly and reaches a peak blood level in 2–4 hours. For treatment of children ages 6–16 having hypertension, the daily dosage range is 1.3–2.7 mg/kg up to a maximum of 160 mg/day. The recommended daily adult dosage range is 80–320 mg/day, given in a single dose. It may take 2–4 weeks for the full therapeutic effect of Diovan to become apparent.

► Tablet form (Novartis): 40 mg (round, yellow); 80 mg (almond-shaped, pale red); 160 mg (almond-shaped, gray-orange); 320 mg (almond-shaped, dark gray-violet). Diovan is also available in combination with the antihypertensive medication hydrochlorothiazide as Diovan HCT in the following dosage strengths: 80/12.5 mg (capsule-shaped, light orange); 160/12.5 mg (capsule-shaped, dark red); 160/25 mg (capsule-shaped brown orange). Tablets identified as 80/12.5, as an example, contain 80 mg of valsartan and 12.5 mg of hydrochlorothiazide.

What is it for?

Doral is used as a short-term treatment for insomnia (i.e., difficulty falling asleep, frequent awakenings, or early awakenings).

What does it do?

It appears that Doral helps induce sleep by blocking the arousal of certain higher functioning brain centers. Doral belongs to the drug class benzodiazepines.

NOTE

Doral is a controlled substance under DEA Schedule IV (see Appendix C). Pregnancy Risk Category X (contraindicated in pregnancy; see Appendix B).

What are the side effects?

Individuals taking Doral may experience a wide range of side effects, including these:

1. Drowsiness/fatigue
2. Headache
3. Irregular heartbeat
4. Dizziness
5. Dry mouth
6. Upset stomach

NOTE

Withdrawal symptoms (cramping, vomiting, convulsions, sweating, etc.) have been reported following abrupt discontinuation of Doral. Individuals who are prone to substance abuse/addiction should be monitored carefully when taking Doral due to the possibility of psychological and physiological dependence.

What are the dosages and forms?

The safety and effectiveness of Doral in children under the age of 18 has not been established. Doral enters the bloodstream rapidly, with peak blood levels occurring within approximately 2 hours. The usual adult dosage range for Doral is 7.5–15 mg/day, given at bedtime.

► Tablet form (Questor): 7.5 mg (capsule-shaped, orange); 15 mg (capsule-shaped, orange). Each tablet is imprinted with the word *DORAL* and the dosage strength.

This fact sheet is not intended to cover all possible medication uses, directions, precautions, drug interactions, or adverse effects and is not a substitute for specific medical advice or to be used as a guide for prescribing.

From *Medication Fact Sheets: A Behavioral Medication Reference for Educators* (3rd ed.), © 2010 by D.E. Konopasek, Champaign IL: Research Press (800-519-2707, www.researchpress.com).

Effexor is available in generic form.

What is it for?

Effexor is an antidepressant used in the treatment of major depressive disorder (MDD) and in preventing the relapse of MDD. Effexor XR is used in the treatment of generalized anxiety disorder (GAD) and social anxiety disorder (social phobia).

What does it do?

Effexor appears to block or inhibit the reabsorption of serotonin and norepinephrine, both central nervous system neurotransmitters. The intended effect is elevation of mood, improved cognitive and psychomotor functioning, and improved concentration.

NOTE

Pregnancy Risk Category C (risk cannot be ruled out; see Appendix B).

What are the side effects?

Individuals taking Effexor may experience a wide range of side effects, including these:

1. Nausea/constipation
2. Headache
3. Loss of appetite
4. Dizziness/drowsiness
5. Anxiety/dry mouth
6. Insomnia

NOTES

▸ It is recommended that Effexor not be taken in combination with monoamine oxidase inhibitors (MAOIs) or within 14 days of discontinuing treatment with an MAOI. At least 7 days should be allowed after stopping Effexor before starting an MAOI.

▸ Individuals taking Effexor should be monitored closely for the potential of worsening depression or the emergence of suicidal thoughts or behavior, particularly in the early stages of medication treatment or when dosages change.

What are the dosages and forms?

The safety of Effexor in children under the age of 18 has not been established. A steady state therapeutic level of Effexor may be observed within 3 days of dosing. The usual therapeutic adult dosage range is 75–225 mg/day, given in two to three divided doses. Some severely depressed individuals may require up to 375 mg/day. Effexor XR is given as a single dose either in the morning or evening.

▸ Tablet form (Wyeth): 25 mg (shield-shaped, peach); 37.5 mg (shield-shaped, peach); 50 mg (shield-shaped, peach); 75 mg (shield-shaped, peach); 100 mg (shield-shaped, peach). Each tablet is inscribed with the dosage.

▸ Extended release capsule form (Wyeth): EFFEXOR XR, 37.5 mg (gray cap, peach body); 75 mg (peach cap, peach body); 150 mg (dark orange cap, dark orange body). Capsules are imprinted with *W* and *Effexor XR* on the cap and the dosage strength on the body.

This fact sheet is not intended to cover all possible medication uses, directions, precautions, drug interactions, or adverse effects and is not a substitute for specific medical advice or to be used as a guide for prescribing.

Eldepryl is available in generic form.

What is it for?

Eldepryl is used in the treatment of Parkinson's disease in conjunction with other anti-Parkinsonian medications.

What does it do?

Eldepryl belongs to a group of antidepressants known as monoamine oxidase inhibitors (MAOIs). Pharmacologically, Eldepryl seems to interfere with the reuptake of the neurotransmitters serotonin and norepinephrine by inhibiting the action of enzymes that normally break down these neurotransmitters.

NOTE

Pregnancy Risk Category C (risk cannot be ruled out; see Appendix B).

What are the side effects?

Individuals taking Eldepryl may experience a wide range of side effects, including these:

1. Nausea
2. Abdominal pain
3. Agitation
4. Insomnia
5. Dizziness/lightheadedness
6. Irregular heartbeat

NOTES

► MAO inhibitors typically require strict dietary management. At dosage levels above 10 mg/day, individuals need to take care to avoid certain foods and beverages, such as beer, red wine, aged cheeses, dry sausage, fava or Italian green beans, brewers' yeast, smoked fish, and liver. This list of food products to be avoided is by no means exhaustive.

► Also, it is very important for individuals taking Eldepryl or other MAOIs not to take other medications without first checking with their physician. Demerol, epinephrine, local anesthetics, many antidepressants, and decongestants may be especially dangerous.

What are the dosages and forms?

The safety and effectiveness of Eldepryl in children has not been established. The recommended maximum adult dosage is 10 mg/day, given in divided doses.

► Capsule form (Somerset): 5 mg (aqua blue cap and body). Capsules are imprinted with *Eldepryl 5 mg.*

This fact sheet is not intended to cover all possible medication uses, directions, precautions, drug interactions, or adverse effects and is not a substitute for specific medical advice or to be used as a guide for prescribing.

From *Medication Fact Sheets: A Behavioral Medication Reference for Educators* (3rd ed.), © 2010 by D.E. Konopasek, Champaign IL: Research Press (800-519-2707, www.researchpress.com).

What is it for?

Felbatol is an anticonvulsant medication used in the treatment of partial seizures. It has also been used in the treatment of Lennox-Gastaut syndrome. Felbatol is rarely used due to the inherent risks of aplastic anemia.

What does it do?

Felbatol appears to reduce seizure activity by suppressing the spread of abnormal or diffuse electrical discharges in the brain and increasing seizure threshold.

NOTE

Pregnancy Risk Category C (risk cannot be ruled out; see Appendix B).

What are the side effects?

Individuals taking Felbatol may experience a wide range of side effects, including these:

1. Loss of appetite
2. Nausea/vomiting
3. Dizziness
4. Headache
5. Insomnia
6. Fatigue

NOTES

► There is a significant risk of developing aplastic anemia, a serious and potentially fatal condition. Additionally, patients taking Felbatol are at high risk for developing serious liver disease. Therefore, Felbatol is only prescribed for patients whose seizure disorder is so severe that the risk of aplastic anemia or liver failure is determined acceptable in light of the benefits to be gained.

► Antiseizure drugs should not be discontinued abruptly due to a risk of increased seizure activity.

What are the dosages and forms?

Felbatol is not recommended for use in children except as a treatment for Lennox-Gastaut syndrome. Felbatol is fairly rapidly absorbed, with a half-life of 20–23 hours. For children ages 2–14 with Lennox-Gastaut syndrome, a maximum daily dosage of 45 mg/kg is recommended. For adults (14 years of age and older), the recommended maximum daily dosage is 3600 mg/day, given in divided doses.

► Tablet form (Medpointe): 400 mg (capsule-shaped, yellow); 600 mg (capsule-shaped, peach).

► Liquid form (Medpointe): Felbatol is available as an oral suspension (600 mg/5 mL).

This fact sheet is not intended to cover all possible medication uses, directions, precautions, drug interactions, or adverse effects and is not a substitute for specific medical advice or to be used as a guide for prescribing.

Fluphenazine is available only in generic form.

What is it for?

Fluphenazine is an antipsychotic medication used in the treatment of schizophrenia.

What does it do?

Fluphenazine has the effect of reducing psychotic symptoms associated with schizophrenia (hallucinations and/or delusions). Fluphenazine seems to act by blocking the action of dopamine, a central nervous system neurotransmitter.

NOTE

Pregnancy Risk Category C (risk cannot be ruled out; see Appendix B).

What are the side effects?

Individuals taking fluphenazine may experience a wide range of side effects, including these:

1. Nausea/loss of appetite
2. Agitation/restlessness
3. Muscle spasms/rigidity
4. Hypertension
5. Dry mouth/blurred vision
6. Tardive dyskinesia/NMS

NOTES

► Tardive dyskinesia is a condition that may develop in individuals of any age group treated with antipsychotic medications for an extended period of time. Symptoms include involuntary movements of the face, tongue, mouth, or jaw and, to a lesser degree, involuntary rhythmic movements of the extremities. There is no known treatment for this condition.

► The medical literature has also reported the occurrence of neuroleptic malignant syndrome (NMS) in individuals taking antipsychotic medication. NMS is a rare but potentially fatal medication reaction involving a range of symptoms, including muscle rigidity, disorientation, irregular pulse and blood pressure, and tachycardia.

► Elderly individuals with dementia-related psychosis are at increased risk of death if treated with antipsychotic drugs and should not take fluphenazine.

What are the dosages and forms?

Fluphenazine is not recommended for children under 12 years of age. The adult dosage range is generally 2–10 mg/day, frequently administered as an intramuscular or subcutaneous injection.

► Tablet form (various pharmaceutical companies): 1 mg; 2.5 mg; 5 mg; 10 mg.

► Liquid form (various pharmaceutical companies): Oral solution concentrate (5 mg/mL); flavored elixir (2.5 mg/5 mL).

► Injection form (various pharmaceutical companies): Fluphenazine is most often administered in long-acting injection form as fluphenazine decanoate. The therapeutic effects of this form of fluphenazine usually become apparent 48–96 hours after injection and may last up to 2 weeks.

From *Medication Fact Sheets: A Behavioral Medication Reference for Educators* (3rd ed.), © 2010 by D.E. Konopasek, Champaign IL: Research Press (800-519-2707, www.researchpress.com).

FOCALIN
(Dexmethylphenidate hydrochloride)

Focalin is available in generic form.

What is it for?

Focalin is used in the treatment of attention-deficit/hyperactivity disorder (ADHD). Its effectiveness for long-term treatment of ADHD (beyond 6 weeks) has not been determined. Therefore, individuals receiving long-term therapy with Focalin should be reevaluated periodically.

What does it do?

Focalin is a central nervous system stimulant. It appears to block the reuptake of norepinephrine and dopamine, both central nervous system neurotransmitters. Stimulants have been shown to be useful in helping individuals improve behaviors commonly associated with ADHD, with effects such as these:

1. Improved motor activity
2. Decreased disruptiveness
3. Improved concentration
4. Improved fine motor coordination
5. More goal-directed behavior
6. Decreased distractibility

NOTE

Focalin is a controlled substance under DEA Schedule II (high potential for abuse; see Appendix C). Pregnancy Risk Category C (risk cannot be ruled out; see Appendix B).

What are the side effects?

Individuals taking Focalin may experience a wide range of side effects, including the following:

1. Loss of appetite/nausea
2. Headache
3. Fever
4. Nervousness/irritability
5. Abdominal pain
6. Tachycardia

NOTES

► Sudden death has been reported in individuals taking stimulant medications who have structural heart defects or other serious heart conditions.

► Medical literature reports that stimulants may intensify the motor and/or vocal tics characteristic of Tourette's syndrome.

► Individuals taking stimulant medications should not take monoamine oxidase inhibitors (MAOIs) at the same time or within 14 days of discontinuing treatment with an MAOI.

► Focalin is not recommended for individuals with glaucoma.

What are the dosages and forms?

Focalin is not recommended for children under 6 years of age. For children 6 years and older, the maximum recommended daily dosage range is 5–20 mg/day, given in divided doses at least 4 hours apart. Generally, doses are adjusted in 2.5–5 mg increments. Focalin is absorbed rapidly, reaching a maximum concentration within about an hour and maintaining a therapeutic effect for several hours. Focalin XR is given as a single dose in the morning. It is absorbed fairly rapidly, with two distinct effect "peaks," the first occurring in approximately 1–2 hours, the second occurring 4.5–7 hours after ingestion.

► Tablet form (Novartis): 2.5 mg (D-shaped, blue); 5 mg (D-shaped, yellow); 10 mg (D-shaped, white).

► Capsule form (Novartis): Focalin XR 5 mg (blue cap, blue body); 10 mg (yellow cap, yellow body); 15 mg (green cap, green body); 20 mg (white cap, white body). Capsules are imprinted with *NVR* along with the dosage strength.

This fact sheet is not intended to cover all possible medication uses, directions, precautions, drug interactions, or adverse effects and is not a substitute for specific medical advice or to be used as a guide for prescribing.

From *Medication Fact Sheets: A Behavioral Medication Reference for Educators* (3rd ed.), © 2010 by D.E. Konopasek, Champaign IL: Research Press (800-519-2707, www.researchpress.com).

What is it for?

Gabitril is an anticonvulsant medication usually used conjunction with other seizure medications in the treatment of partial seizure disorders.

What does it do?

The precise mechanism through which Gabitril works is unknown, although it is believed to enhance the availability of the neurotransmitter GABA (gamma aminobutyric acid) by blocking its reuptake, which helps inhibit or slow down activity in certain parts of the brain.

NOTE

Pregnancy Risk Category C (risk cannot be ruled out; see Appendix B).

What are the side effects?

Individuals taking Gabitril may experience a wide range of side effects, including these:

1. Dizziness/lightheadedness
2. Lack of energy
3. Nausea/abdominal pain
4. Difficulty concentrating
5. Tremors
6. Nervousness/irritability

NOTES

- Antiseizure drugs should not be discontinued abruptly due to a risk of increased seizure activity.
- There is an increased risk of seizures in patients without epilepsy being treated with Gabitril.

What are the dosages and forms?

Gabitril is generally administered with other anticonvulsant drugs. It enters the bloodstream fairly rapidly (approximately 45 minutes) but may take 2 days to achieve a steady therapeutic blood level with multiple doses. In adolescents ages 12–18, the recommended initial dose is 4 mg given once daily. Over a period of weeks, the total daily dosage for this age group may reach 32 mg/day, given in two to four doses. For adults, the recommended initial dose is 4 mg/day, given in a single dose. Over a period of weeks, the recommended dose may be increased incrementally to a maximum of 56 mg/day, given in two to four divided doses.

- Tablet form (Cepahlon): 2 mg (round, orange-peach); 4 mg (round, yellow); 12 mg (oval, green); 16 mg (oval, blue); 20 mg (oval, pink). Tablets are debossed with a *C* on one side and *402, 404, 412,* or *416* on the other, depending on the dosage.

This fact sheet is not intended to cover all possible medication uses, directions, precautions, drug interactions, or adverse effects and is not a substitute for specific medical advice or to be used as a guide for prescribing.

From *Medication Fact Sheets: A Behavioral Medication Reference for Educators* (3rd ed.), © 2010 by D.E. Konopasek, Champaign IL: Research Press (800-519-2707, www.researchpress.com).

GEODON   (Ziprasidone hydrochloride)

What is it for?

Geodon is an antipsychotic medication used in the treatment of psychotic disorders. It is also approved for treatment of acute manic or mixed episodes associated with bipolar disorder. Geodon is typically not the medication of first choice for individuals with cardiac irregularities.

What does it do?

Pharmacologically, Geodon appears to block the neurotransmitters dopamine and serotonin. It has the effect of reducing psychotic symptoms (delusions and/or hallucinations) associated with schizophrenia.

NOTE

Pregnancy Risk Category C (risk cannot be ruled out; see Appendix B).

What are the side effects?

Individuals taking Geodon may experience a wide range of side effects, including these:

1. Rash
2. Sleepiness
3. Cardiac arrhythmias
4. Tremors/shakiness
5. Flu-like symptoms
6. Tardive dyskinesia/NMS

NOTES

► The medical literature reports a risk of potentially fatal cardiac arrhythmias associated with Geodon.

► Tardive dyskinesia is a condition that may develop in individuals of any age group treated with antipsychotic medications for an extended period of time. Symptoms include involuntary movements of the face, tongue, mouth, or jaw and, to a lesser degree, involuntary rhythmic movements of the extremities. There is no known treatment for this condition.

► The medical literature has also reported the occurrence of neuroleptic malignant syndrome (NMS) in individuals taking antipsychotic medication. NMS is a rare but potentially fatal medication reaction involving a range of symptoms, including muscle rigidity, disorientation, irregular pulse and blood pressure, and tachycardia.

► There is an increased risk of death in elderly individuals with dementia-related psychosis who are being treated with Geodon.

► There is a risk of developing hyperglycemia and diabetes mellitus in individuals treated with atypical antipsychotic medications, including Geodon.

What are the dosages and forms?

The safety and effectiveness of Geodon in children has not been studied. The recommended daily adult dose is 20–80 mg, given in two doses. Geodon is fairly rapidly absorbed, reaching peak plasma concentrations in 6–8 hours. Steady state concentrations are reached in 1–3 days.

► Capsule form (Pfizer): 20 mg (white cap, blue body); 40 mg (blue cap, blue body); 60 mg (white cap, white body); 80 mg (white cap, blue body).

► Injection form (Pfizer): Geodon is available as an intramuscular injection, 20 mg/mL.

This fact sheet is not intended to cover all possible medication uses, directions, precautions, drug interactions, or adverse effects and is not a substitute for specific medical advice or to be used as a guide for prescribing.

From *Medication Fact Sheets: A Behavioral Medication Reference for Educators* (3rd ed.), © 2010 by D.E. Konopasek, Champaign IL: Research Press (800-519-2707, www.researchpress.com).

Halcion is available in generic form.

What is it for?

Halcion is used as a short-term treatment of insomnia (7–10 days). Insomnia includes difficulty falling asleep, frequent awakenings, or early awakenings.

What does it do?

Halcion is a central nervous system depressant and helps induce sleep by blocking the arousal of certain higher functioning brain centers. Halcion belongs to the drug class benzodiazepine. Long-term use is not recommended.

NOTE

Halcion is a controlled substance under DEA Schedule IV (see Appendix C). Pregnancy Risk Category X (contraindicated in pregnancy; see Appendix B).

What are the side effects?

Individuals taking Halcion may experience a wide variety of side effects, including these:

1. Drowsiness
2. Dizziness
3. Nervousness
4. Nausea/vomiting
5. Impaired coordination
6. Lightheadedness

NOTE

Withdrawal symptoms (cramping, vomiting, convulsions, sweating, etc.) have been reported following abrupt discontinuation of Halcion. Individuals who are prone to substance abuse/addiction should be monitored carefully when taking Halcion due to the possibility of psychological and physiological dependence.

What are the dosages and forms?

The usefulness of Halcion in children under the age of 18 has not been determined. In adults, a bedtime dose of 0.125–0.25 mg is generally sufficient. Doses above 0.5 mg are not recommended. Halcion enters the bloodstream relatively rapidly, with peak blood levels occurring approximately 2 hours after ingestion.

► Tablet form (Pharmacia and Upjohn): 0.125 mg (oval, white); 0.25 mg (oval, light blue). Tablets are scored and imprinted with the word *HALCION* and the dosage.

This fact sheet is not intended to cover all possible medication uses, directions, precautions, drug interactions, or adverse effects and is not a substitute for specific medical advice or to be used as a guide for prescribing.

Oral Haldol is now available only as generic haloperidol.

What is it for?

Haldol is used to treat psychotic disorders as well as severe behavior problems such as aggression. It has also been used effectively to treat tic disorders and vocal utterances associated with Tourette's syndrome.

What does it do?

Haldol helps decrease psychotic symptoms such as hallucinations and delusions. Pharmacologically, Haldol appears to block the effects of dopamine, a central nervous system neurotransmitter.

NOTE

Pregnancy Risk Category C (risk cannot be ruled out; see Appendix B).

What are the side effects?

Individuals taking Haldol may experience a wide range of side effects, including these:

1. Tremors/shakiness
2. Blurred vision
3. Dystonic reactions (marked arching of back, eyes rolling upward)
4. Dry mouth
5. Urinary retention
6. Tardive dyskinesia/NMS

NOTES

► Tardive dyskinesia is a condition that may develop in individuals of any age group treated with antipsychotic medications for an extended period of time. Symptoms include involuntary movements of the face, tongue, mouth, or jaw and, to a lesser degree, involuntary rhythmic movements of the extremities. There is no known treatment for this condition.

► The medical literature has also reported the occurrence of neuroleptic malignant syndrome (NMS) in individuals taking antipsychotic medication.

NMS is a rare but potentially fatal medication reaction involving a range of symptoms, including muscle rigidity, disorientation, irregular pulse and blood pressure, and tachycardia.

► There is an increased risk of death in elderly individuals with dementia-related psychosis who are being treated with Haldol.

► Individuals taking both Haldol and Lithium should be monitored closely due to the possibility of developing serious, potentially irreversible brain damage.

What are the dosages and forms?

For children ages 3–12 (weight range 15–40 kg) the dosage may range from 0.05 mg/kg/day to 0.075 mg/kg/day. For children with psychotic disorders, the dosage may be somewhat higher. Adults showing severe symptomology may require 3–5 mg two to three times per day.

► Tablet form (various pharmaceutical companies): 0.5 mg; 1 mg; 2 mg; 5 mg; 10 mg; 20 mg. Tablets are available only as generic haloperidol.

► Liquid form (various pharmaceutical companies): Haloperidol is available as a liquid concentrate (2 mg/mL).

► Injection form (Ortho-McNeil): Haldol is available in injectable form as Haldol or Haldol Decanoate (long-acting form of Haldol). Injectable generic haloperidol is available through various pharmaceutical companies.

This fact sheet is not intended to cover all possible medication uses, directions, precautions, drug interactions, or adverse effects and is not a substitute for specific medical advice or to be used as a guide for prescribing.

From *Medication Fact Sheets: A Behavioral Medication Reference for Educators* (3rd ed.), © 2010 by D.E. Konopasek, Champaign IL: Research Press (800-519-2707, www.researchpress.com).

Inderal is available in generic form. INNOPRAN XL is another trade name for propranolol.

What is it for?

Inderal is an antihypertensive medication used in the treatment of high blood pressure. It is also used in the long-term management of individuals with cardiac arrhythmias (irregular heartbeat), as a treatment for rage reactions associated with brain injury, and as a preventative treatment for common migraine headaches.

What does it do?

Inderal belongs to a class of drugs known as beta-blockers. As such, it has the effect of lowering blood pressure, lowering heart rate, and stabilizing cardiac functioning. It acts to reduce symptoms of anxiety by blocking certain neural pathways in the brain. It reduces the oxygen requirement of the heart and helps stabilize the heartbeat.

NOTE

Pregnancy Risk Category C (risk cannot be ruled out; see Appendix B).

What are the side effects?

Individuals taking Inderal may experience a wide range of side effects, including these:

1. Lightheadedness
2. Nausea/vomiting
3. Insomnia
4. Mental depression
5. Weakness/fatigue

NOTE

Inderal should not be discontinued abruptly, especially in individuals with a history of severe chest pain (angina pectoris) due to the risk of heart attack.

What are the dosages and forms?

The usual adult dosage for individuals with hypertension is 120–240 mg/day, given in divided doses. Peak effects of occur within about 1–2 hours and remain at a therapeutic level for approximately 4 hours. Inderal is available in a sustained release form called Inderal LA. Peak effects for Inderal LA occur approximately 6 hours after ingestion.

- Tablet form (Watson): 10 mg (round, orange); 20 mg (round, blue); 40 mg (round, green); 80 mg (round, yellow).

- Sustained release capsule form (Akrimax): Inderal LA, 60 mg (light blue and white cap, light blue body); 80 mg (light blue cap, light blue body); 120 mg (dark blue cap, light blue body); 160 mg (dark blue cap, dark blue body).

- Injection form (various pharmaceutical companies): Inderal is available as an intramuscular injection, 1 mg/mL.

This fact sheet is not intended to cover all possible medication uses, directions, precautions, drug interactions, or adverse effects and is not a substitute for specific medical advice or to be used as a guide for prescribing.

What is it for?

Invega is an atypical antipsychotic medication used in the treatment of schizophrenia.

What does it do?

Invega acts to improve cognitive functioning and mood as well as reducing psychotic symptoms associated with schizophrenia (delusions and hallucinations). Pharmacologically, it appears primarily to block the effects of dopamine and serotonin, both central nervous system neurotransmitters.

NOTE

Pregnancy Risk Category C (risk cannot be ruled out; see Appendix B).

What are the side effects?

Individuals taking Invega may experience a wide range of side effects, including these:

1. Dizziness when standing up
2. Headache
3. Nausea/vomiting
4. Irregular heartbeat
5. Insomnia
6. Tardive dyskinesia/NMS

NOTE

► Tardive dyskinesia is a condition that may develop in individuals of any age group treated with antipsychotic medications for an extended period of time. Symptoms include involuntary movements of the face, tongue, mouth, or jaw and, to a lesser degree, involuntary rhythmic movements of the extremities. There is no known treatment for this condition.

► The medical literature has also reported the occurrence of neuroleptic malignant syndrome (NMS) in individuals taking antipsychotic medication. NMS is a rare but potentially fatal medication reaction involving a range of symptoms, including muscle rigidity, disorientation, irregular pulse and blood pressure, and tachycardia.

► Elderly individuals with dementia-related psychosis are at increased risk of death if treated with antipsychotic drugs and should not take Invega.

► There is a risk of developing hyperglycemia and diabetes mellitus in individuals treated with atypical antipsychotic medications, including Invega.

What are the dosages and forms?

The safety and effectiveness of Invega in children and adolescents under the age of 18 has not been established. Invega reaches peak concentration levels approximately 24 hours after ingestion, with steady state levels occurring in approximately 4–5 days. The recommended adult dosage range is 6–12 mg, given once daily.

► Tablet form (Ortho-McNeil-Janssen): 6 mg (round, beige); 9 mg (round, pink).

This fact sheet is not intended to cover all possible medication uses, directions, precautions, drug interactions, or adverse effects and is not a substitute for specific medical advice or to be used as a guide for prescribing.

From *Medication Fact Sheets: A Behavioral Medication Reference for Educators* (3rd ed.), © 2010 by D.E. Konopasek, Champaign IL: Research Press (800-519-2707, www.researchpress.com).

Klonopin is available in generic form.

What is it for?

Klonopin is useful in the treatment of certain types of seizure disorders (petit mal, akinetic, and myoclonic seizures). It is also recognized as a treatment for panic disorders.

What does it do?

Klonopin is a central nervous system depressant and appears to suppress some spike and wave activity in the brain, thereby decreasing the intensity of some forms of seizure disorder, particularly absence seizures (petit mal). Klonopin belongs to the drug class benzodiazepine.

NOTE

Klonopin is a controlled substance under DEA Schedule IV (see Appendix C). Pregnancy Risk Category D (positive evidence of risk; see Appendix B).

What are the side effects?

Individuals taking Klonopin may experience a wide range of side effects, including these:

1. Sedation
2. Difficulty with motor tasks
3. Decreased coordination
4. Irritability
5. Confusion
6. Abnormal eye movements

NOTES

► Withdrawal symptoms (cramping, vomiting, convulsions, sweating, etc.) have been reported following abrupt discontinuation of Klonopin. Individuals who are prone to substance abuse/addiction should be monitored carefully when taking Klonopin due to the possibility for psychological and physiological dependence.

► Antiseizure drugs should not be discontinued abruptly due to a risk of increased seizure activity.

What are the dosages and forms?

The safety of Klonopin as a treatment for panic disorder in individuals under the age of 18 has not been established. For the treatment of seizures, the maximum recommended maintenance dose for children up to age 10 is 0.1–0.2 mg/kg/day, given in two to three divided doses The maximum recommended dose for adults is 20 mg/day. Peak blood levels of Klonopin typically occur within 1–4 hours after ingestion and maintain a therapeutic blood level for approximately 30–40 hours.

► Tablet form (Roche): 0.5 mg (round, orange); 1 mg (round, blue); 2 mg (round, white). Tablets have the letter *K* perforated in the center along with the dosage embossed.

► Wafer form (Roche): Klonopin is available as an orally disintegrating wafer. 0.125 mg (round, white); 0.25 mg (round white); 0.5 mg (round, white); 1 mg (round, white); 2 mg (round, white).

This fact sheet is not intended to cover all possible medication uses, directions, precautions, drug interactions, or adverse effects and is not a substitute for specific medical advice or to be used as a guide for prescribing.

Lamictal is available in generic form.

What is it for?

Lamictal is an anticonvulsant usually used in combination with other anticonvulsant medications to control partial seizures and generalized seizures of Lennox-Gastaut syndrome. It has also been used as maintenance treatment for bipolar disorder to delay the time between mood episodes.

What does it do?

The exact mechanism of Lamictal's action is not known. It is presumed that Lamictal reduces the spread of seizure activity and stabilizes brain activity associated with seizures.

NOTE

Pregnancy Risk Category C (risk cannot be ruled out; see Appendix B).

What are the side effects?

Individuals taking Lamictal may experience a wide range of side effects, including these:

1. Headache
2. Dizziness
3. Blurred vision
4. Nausea/vomiting
5. Drowsiness
6. Skin rash

NOTES

► Lamictal is associated with a rare but potentially life-threatening skin rash. Approximately 1 in 1,000 adults develop this rash. In children, the risk is much greater. The use of Lamictal in children under the age of 16 is not approved, unless they have seizures associated with Lennox-Gastaut syndrome.

► Antiseizure drugs should not be discontinued abruptly due to a risk of increased seizure activity.

What are the dosages and forms?

Lamictal enters the bloodstream fairly quickly, with peak blood levels observed within 1–4 hours after ingestion. Since Lamictal is generally prescribed in combination with other drugs, the maximum recommended dosage may vary depending on which other medications are used in conjunction.

► Tablet form (GlaxoSmithKline): 25 mg (shield-shaped, white); 100 mg (shield-shaped, peach); 150 mg (shield-shaped, cream); 200 mg (shield-shaped, blue). Tablets are imprinted with the word *LAMICTAL* and the dosage.

► Lamictal is also available in chewable tablet form (GlaxoSmithKline): 2 mg (round, white); 5 mg (capsule-shaped, white); 25 mg (square, white).

Lexapro is available in generic form.

What is it for?

Lexapro is an antidepressant used in the treatment of major depressive disorder (MDD) and generalized anxiety disorder (GAD).

What does it do?

Lexapro belongs to a group of antidepressants known as selective serotonin reuptake inhibitors (SSRIs). As such, it acts to block or inhibit the reabsorption of serotonin, a central nervous system neurotransmitter. The intended effect is elevation of mood, improved cognitive and psychomotor functioning, and improved concentration.

NOTE

Pregnancy Risk Category C (risk cannot be ruled out; see Appendix B).

What are the side effects?

Individuals taking Lexapro may experience a wide range of side effects, including these:

1. Dry mouth
2. Nausea/vomiting
3. Diarrhea
4. Insomnia
5. Increased sweating
6. Dizziness

NOTES

- It is recommended that Lexapro not be taken in combination with monoamine oxidase inhibitors (MAOIs) or within 14 days of discontinuing treatment with an MAOI. At least 14 days should be allowed after stopping Lexapro before starting an MAOI.

- Individuals taking Lexapro should be monitored closely for the potential of worsening depression or the emergence of suicidal thoughts or behavior, particularly in the early stages of medication treatment or when dosages change.

- A serious, potentially life-threatening condition known as serotonin syndrome can occur when SSRIs and certain medications used to treat migraine headaches (triptans) are taken together.

What are the dosages and forms?

The safety and effectiveness of Lexapro in children has not been clinically established. Lexapro is absorbed fairly slowly, reaching peak blood levels in about 5 hours. A therapeutic steady state is typically reached in approximately one week. The usual initial adult dosage is 10 mg/day, given in a single dose. After a minimum of 1 week, the dosage may be increased to 20 mg/day. For individuals over the age of 60 or for those with liver disease, a dosage over 10 mg/day is not recommended.

- Tablet form (Forest): 5 mg (round, white); 10 mg (round, white); 20 mg (round, white). Tablets are scored and imprinted with *FL* on the scored side and the dosage strength on the other side.

- Liquid form (Forest): Lexapro is also available as an oral solution (5 mg/5 mL).

This fact sheet is not intended to cover all possible medication uses, directions, precautions, drug interactions, or adverse effects and is not a substitute for specific medical advice or to be used as a guide for prescribing.

From *Medication Fact Sheets: A Behavioral Medication Reference for Educators* (3rd ed.), © 2010 by D.E. Konopasek, Champaign IL: Research Press (800-519-2707, www.researchpress.com).

Librium is available in generic form.

What is it for?

Librium is primarily used to treat anxiety and tension. It is also used to reduce symptoms associated with alcohol withdrawal.

What does it do?

Librium is a central nervous system depressant. The precise action is not known, but it seems to block arousal at the brain stem. Librium belongs to the drug class benzodiazepine.

NOTE

Librium is a controlled substance under DEA Schedule IV (see Appendix C). Pregnancy Risk Category D (positive evidence of risk; see Appendix B).

What are the side effects?

Individuals taking Librium may experience a wide range of side effects, including these:

1. Drowsiness
2. Nausea
3. Skin rash
4. Confusion
5. Constipation
6. Decreased motor control

NOTE

Withdrawal symptoms (cramping, vomiting, convulsions, sweating, etc.) have been reported following abrupt discontinuation of Librium. Individuals who are prone to substance abuse/addiction should be monitored carefully when taking Librium due to the possibility for psychological and physiological dependence.

What are the dosages and forms?

The use of Librium in children under the age of 6 is not recommended. For children over 6 years of age, the typical maximum daily dosage is 10–30 mg/day, given in two to four divided doses. The maximum adult dosage for Librium may reach 100 mg/day for the relief of severe anxiety disorders. It takes approximately 2 hours for peak blood levels to be reached after ingestion. Librium maintains its therapeutic effect for 4–6 hours.

▸ Capsule form (Valeant): 5 mg (light green cap, yellow body); 10 mg (black cap, light green body); 25 mg (light green cap, white body).

This fact sheet is not intended to cover all possible medication uses, directions, precautions, drug interactions, or adverse effects and is not a substitute for specific medical advice or to be used as a guide for prescribing.

From *Medication Fact Sheets: A Behavioral Medication Reference for Educators* (3rd ed.), © 2010 by D.E. Konopasek, Champaign IL: Research Press (800-519-2707, www.researchpress.com).

Limbitrol is available in generic form.

What is it for?

Limbitrol combines the antianxiety agent chlordiazepoxide (Librium) with the tricyclic antidepressant amitriptyline. Limbitrol is used to treat individuals who have moderate to severe depression along with moderate to severe anxiety.

What does it do?

Limbitrol acts as both a central nervous system depressant (benzodiazepine), which has the effect of reducing anxiety and tension, and a tricyclic antidepressant, which appears to block the reuptake of norepinephrine, a central nervous system neurotransmitter.

NOTE

Limbitrol is a controlled substance under DEA Schedule IV (see Appendix C). Pregnancy Risk Category D (positive evidence of risk; see Appendix B).

What are the side effects?

Individuals taking Limbitrol may experience a wide range of side effects, including these:

1. Drowsiness
2. Constipation
3. Dizziness
4. Dry mouth
5. Blurred vision
6. Bloating

NOTES

► Individuals with angle-closure glaucoma taking Limbitrol should be monitored closely due to increased risk of visual crisis.

► Individuals taking Limbitrol should be monitored closely for the potential of worsening depression or the emergence of suicidal thoughts or behavior, particularly in the early stages of medication treatment or when dosages change.

What are the dosages and forms?

The use of Limbitrol in children under the age of 12 has not been studied sufficiently to determine its safety. The usual adult dosage is 10 mg chlordiazepoxide and 25 mg amitriptyline given 3–4 times per day to a maximum of 6 times per day.

► Tablet form (Valeant): Limbitrol DS (double-strength), 10 mg chlordiazepoxide and 25 mg amitriptyline (round, white). Limbitrol, 5 mg chlordiazepoxide and 12.5 mg amitriptyline (round, blue).

This fact sheet is not intended to cover all possible medication uses, directions, precautions, drug interactions, or adverse effects and is not a substitute for specific medical advice or to be used as a guide for prescribing.

From *Medication Fact Sheets: A Behavioral Medication Reference for Educators* (3rd ed.), © 2010 by D.E. Konopasek, Champaign IL: Research Press (800-519-2707, www.researchpress.com).

Lithium is available in generic form. ESKALITH, ESKALITH CR, LITHOBID, LITHONATE, and LITHOTABS are other brand names for Lithium carbonate.

What is it for?

Lithium is a mood stabilizing medication used in the treatment of manic episodes in individuals with bipolar disorder. It has also been used to treat episodic anger and/or aggression, schizophrenia, and certain depressive disorders.

What does it do?

Lithium has the effect of diminishing the intensity of episodes of mania in individuals with a history of bipolar disorder. Manic behavior may include: (a) pressured speech, (b) hyperactivity, (c) reduced need for sleep, (d) grandiosity, (e) poor judgment, and (f) aggression and/or hostility. Lithium may increase the reuptake of serotonin and norepinephrine, although the precise mechanism is unclear.

NOTE

Pregnancy Risk Category D (positive evidence of risk; see Appendix B).

What are the side effects?

Individuals taking Lithium may experience a wide range of side effects, including these:

1. Nausea/vomiting/abdominal pain
2. Diarrhea
3. Slowed thinking
4. Tremor (especially in fingers)
5. Decreased memory
6. Weight gain

NOTE

Lithium is generally not recommended for individuals with liver or heart disease, since the risk of lithium toxicity is very high.

What are the dosages and forms?

Lithium is not recommended for children under the age of 12 since its safety and effectiveness with this age group has not been clinically determined. Although dosages vary, the usual maintenance adult dose of Lithium is 600–1200 mg/day, given in divided doses. Peak blood levels are generally reached within about 3 hours after the last dose. It may take 1–3 weeks to normalize manic symptoms in adults.

NOTE

Lithium has a very narrow therapeutic range. Therefore, blood levels should be closely monitored.

► Tablet form (Roxane): 300 mg (round, white). Sustained release (SR) tablet form (Glaxo-SmithKline): Eskalith CR, 450 mg (round, yellow); Lithobid (Noven), 300 mg (round, peach). Extended release tablet form (Roxane), 300 mg (round, beige); 450 mg (round, white).

► Capsule form (GlaxoSmithKline): Eskalith, 300 mg (gray cap, yellow body). (Roxane), 150 mg (white cap, white body); 300 mg (beige cap, beige body); 600 mg (beige cap, white body).

► Liquid form: Lithium is also available in syrup form, 8 mEq/5 mL

Loxapine is available only in generic form.

What is it for?

Loxapine is an antipsychotic medication used in the treatment of psychotic disorders.

What does it do?

Loxapine aids in reducing psychotic symptoms associated with schizophrenia (hallucinations and/or delusions). It also exerts a calming effect and suppresses aggressive behavior.

NOTE

Pregnancy Risk Category C (risk cannot be ruled out; see Appendix B).

What are the side effects?

Individuals taking Loxapine may experience a wide range of side effects, including these:

1. Mild sedation/fatigue
2. Agitation/restlessness
3. Tremors/shakiness
4. Hypotension/dizziness
5. Dry mouth/blurred vision
6. Tardive dyskinesia/NMS

NOTES

► Tardive dyskinesia is a condition that may develop in individuals of any age group treated with antipsychotic medications for an extended period of time. Symptoms include involuntary movements of the face, tongue, mouth, or jaw and, to a lesser degree, involuntary rhythmic movements of the extremities. There is no known treatment for this condition.

► The medical literature has also reported the occurrence of neuroleptic malignant syndrome (NMS) in individuals taking antipsychotic medication. NMS is a rare but potentially fatal medication reaction involving a range of symptoms, including muscle rigidity, disorientation, irregular pulse and blood pressure, and tachycardia.

► Loxapine lowers the convulsive seizure threshold and therefore should be used with caution in individuals with seizure disorders.

What are the dosages and forms?

Due to a lack of clinical studies, Loxapine is not recommended for children under the age of 16. It is rapidly absorbed, with initial effects observed within 30 minutes and effects lasting 12 hours or more. Loxapine is usually administered in divided doses two to four times per day. The typical therapeutic dosage range for adults is 60–100 mg/day.

► Capsule form (Watson): 5 mg (white cap, white body); 10 mg (yellow cap, white body); 25 mg (green cap, white body); 50 mg (blue cap, white body).

From *Medication Fact Sheets: A Behavioral Medication Reference for Educators* (3rd ed.), © 2010 by D.E. Konopasek, Champaign IL: Research Press (800-519-2707, www.researchpress.com).

Luvox is available in generic form.

What is it for?

Although Luvox is classified as an antidepressant, it is used primarily as a treatment for social anxiety disorder (SAD) and obsessive-compulsive disorder (OCD).

What does it do?

Luvox belongs to a group of antidepressants known as selective serotonin reuptake inhibitors (SSRIs). As such, it acts to block or inhibit the reabsorption of serotonin, a central nervous system neurotransmitter. The intended effect is an elevation of mood, improved cognitive and psychomotor functioning, and improved concentration. Luvox has the effect of weakening obsessive and compulsive behavior patterns.

NOTE

Pregnancy Risk Category C (risk cannot be ruled out; see Appendix B).

What are the side effects?

Individuals taking Luvox may experience a wide range of side effects, including these:

1. Nausea/vomiting
2. Headache
3. Drowsiness
4. Constipation
5. Loss of appetite
6. Dizziness

NOTES

- It is recommended that Luvox not be taken in combination with monoamine oxidase inhibitors (MAOIs) or within 14 days of discontinuing treatment with an MAOI. At least 14 days should be allowed after stopping Luvox before starting an MAOI.

- Individuals taking Luvox should be monitored closely for the potential of worsening depression or the emergence of suicidal thoughts or behavior, particularly in the early stages of medication treatment or when dosages change.

- A serious, potentially life-threatening condition known as serotonin syndrome can occur when SSRIs and certain medications used to treat migraine headaches (triptans) are taken together.

What are the dosages and forms?

Luvox has not been evaluated in children. The usual adult dosage range is 100–300 mg/day, given once daily. It may take a week to reach a steady state therapeutic level.

- Capsule form (Jazz): Luvox CR, 100 mg (dark blue cap, white body); 150 mg (dark blue cap, light blue body).

- Tablet form (various pharmaceutical companies): 25 mg; 50 mg; 100 mg. Tablets are round or ovoid. Colors may vary depending on manufacturer

What is it for?

Marplan is used in the treatment of depression. It is rarely used as the first treatment of choice for major depressive disorder (MDD) but may be prescribed for individuals who do not respond to other types of antidepressants or who have atypical depression.

What does it do?

Marplan belongs to a group of antidepressants known as monoamine oxidase inhibitors (MAOIs). Pharmacologically, Marplan seems to interfere with the reuptake of the neurotransmitters serotonin and norepinephrine by inhibiting the action of enzymes that normally break down these neurotransmitters.

NOTE

Pregnancy Risk Category C (risk cannot be ruled out; see Appendix B).

What are the side effects?

Individuals taking Marplan may experience a wide range of side effects, including these:

1. Dizziness
2. Headache
3. Dry mouth
4. Constipation
5. Nausea
6. Hypertensive crisis

NOTES

► Hypertensive crisis can be fatal. Marplan, along with other MAOIs, requires strict dietary vigilance. Individuals taking Marplan should take great care to avoid certain foods and beverages, such as beer, red wine, aged cheeses, dry sausage, fava or Italian green beans, brewers' yeast, smoked fish, and liver. This list of food products to be avoided is by no means exhaustive.

► Also, it is very important for individuals taking Marplan or other MAOIs not to take other medications without first checking with their physician.

Demerol, epinephrine, local anesthetics, many antidepressants, and decongestants may be especially dangerous.

► Individuals taking Marplan should be monitored closely for the potential of worsening depression or the emergence of suicidal thoughts or behavior, particularly in the early stages of medication treatment or when dosages change.

What are the dosages and forms?

Marplan is not recommended for individuals under the age of 16. The typical adult dosage is 40–60 mg/day, administered in two to four doses.

► Tablet form (Validus): 10 mg (round, peach).

This fact sheet is not intended to cover all possible medication uses, directions, precautions, drug interactions, or adverse effects and is not a substitute for specific medical advice or to be used as a guide for prescribing.

From *Medication Fact Sheets: A Behavioral Medication Reference for Educators* (3rd ed.), © 2010 by D.E. Konopasek, Champaign IL: Research Press (800-519-2707, www.researchpress.com).

Mebaral is available in generic form.

What is it for?

Mebaral is a sedative and is used to relieve anxiety, tension, and apprehension. It has also been used to treat sleep disturbances (insomnia) as well as grand mal and petit mal epilepsy.

What does it do?

Mebaral is a barbiturate and acts to depress sensory activity within the brain. It also decreases motor activity and produces a calming effect. As an anticonvulsant, Mebaral tends to be less sedating than phenobarbital.

NOTE

Mebaral is a controlled substance under DEA Schedule IV (see Appendix C). Pregnancy Risk Category D (positive evidence of risk; see Appendix B).

What are the side effects?

Individuals taking Mebaral may experience a wide range of side effects, including these:

1. Drowsiness
2. Dizziness
3. Stomach upset
4. Agitation/confusion
5. Weakness
6. Headache

NOTES

▸ Individuals should avoid using alcohol while taking Mebaral. Also, individuals prone to addiction or drug dependence should be monitored closely when taking Mebaral due to the risk of psychological and physiological dependence.

▸ Antiseizure drugs should not be discontinued abruptly due to a risk of increased seizure activity.

What are the dosages and forms?

As a treatment for seizure disorder, the typical dosage range for children under the age of 5 is 16–32 mg given three to four times per day. For children over 5 years of age, the dosage range is 32–64 mg given three to four times per day. The recommended adult dosage is 400–600 mg/day, given in divided doses. Mebaral is rapidly absorbed into the bloodstream, with effects generally noticed within 30–60 minutes following ingestion and effects lasting 10–16 hours.

▸ Tablet form (Ovation): 32 mg (1/2 grain, white, round); 50 mg (3/4 grain, white, round); 100 mg (1 1/2 grain, white, round).

From *Medication Fact Sheets: A Behavioral Medication Reference for Educators* (3rd ed.), © 2010 by D.E. Konopasek, Champaign IL: Research Press (800-519-2707, www.researchpress.com).

Meprobamate   (formerly MILTOWN or EQUANIL)

Meprobamate is available only in generic form.
Meprobamate is an antianxiety medication useful in the short-term (less than 4 months) treatment of anxiety disorders and hypertension. It also has muscle relaxing and sedative effects.

What does it do?

Meprobamate acts on the limbic system and the thalamus to relax skeletal muscles, thereby exerting a calming effect.

NOTE

Meprobamate is a controlled substance under DEA Schedule IV (see Appendix C). Pregnancy Risk Category D (positive evidence of risk; see Appendix B).

What are the side effects?

Individuals taking meprobamate may experience a wide range of side effects, including these:

1. Sedation
2. Dizziness
3. Slurred speech
4. Poor coordination
5. Nausea
6. Palpitations

NOTE

Withdrawal symptoms (cramping, vomiting, convulsions, sweating, etc.) have been reported following abrupt discontinuation of meprobamate. Individuals who are prone to substance abuse/addiction should be monitored carefully when taking meprobamate due to the possibility for psychological and physiological dependence.

What are the dosages and forms?

The use of meprobamate for children under the age of 6 is not recommended. The typical dose for children ages 6–12 is 200–600 mg/day, given in divided doses. The clinical dose of meprobamate in adults is generally 400 mg given three to four times per day to a maximum of 2400 mg/day. It is recommended that meprobamate be discontinued after 4 months.

► Tablet form (Watson): 200 mg (round, white); 400 mg (round, white).

This fact sheet is not intended to cover all possible medication uses, directions, precautions, drug interactions, or adverse effects and is not a substitute for specific medical advice or to be used as a guide for prescribing.

From *Medication Fact Sheets: A Behavioral Medication Reference for Educators* (3rd ed.), © 2010 by D.E. Konopasek, Champaign IL: Research Press (800-519-2707, www.researchpress.com).

Methylphenidate is available in generic form.

What is it for?

Metadate is most often used as a treatment for attention-deficit/hyperactivity disorder (ADHD).

What does it do?

Metadate is a central nervous system stimulant. It appears to block the reuptake of norepinephrine and dopamine, both central nervous system neurotransmitters. It has been shown to be useful in helping individuals improve behaviors commonly associated with ADHD, with effects such as these:

1. Improved motor activity
2. Decreased disruptiveness
3. Improved fine motor coordination
4. More goal-directed behavior
5. Decreased distractibility
6. Improved concentration

NOTE

Metadate is a controlled substance under DEA Schedule II (high potential for abuse; see Appendix C). Pregnancy Risk Category C (risk cannot be ruled out; see Appendix B).

What are the side effects?

Individuals taking Metadate may experience a wide range of side effects, including these:

1. Loss of appetite
2. Insomnia
3. Upset stomach
4. Headache/dizziness
5. Rash
6. Tachycardia

NOTES

- Sudden death has been reported in individuals taking stimulant medications who have structural heart defects or other serious heart conditions.

- Medical literature reports that stimulants may intensify the motor and/or vocal tics characteristic of Tourette's syndrome.

- Individuals taking stimulant medications should not take monoamine oxidase inhibitors (MAOIs) at the same time or within 14 days of discontinuing treatment with an MAOI.

- Metadate should not be used in individuals with glaucoma.

What are the dosages and forms?

Metadate is quickly absorbed, with two effect peaks, the first occurring within approximately 1.5 hours and the second occurring 4–5 hours after ingestion. Metadate has a duration of action of approximately 8 hours, after which the effect gradually weakens. Metadate has not been studied in children under the age of 6. The typical adult dosage is 20–60 mg/day. In children over the age of 6, a dosage higher than 60 mg/day is not recommended. Metadate is useful when a single long-lasting dose is preferable to two or more doses of the immediate release tablet form of methylphenidate.

- Tablet form (UCB): Metadate ER (extended release). 10 mg (white, oval); 20 mg (white, round).

- Capsule form (UCB): Metadate CD (controlled release); 10 mg (green cap, white body); 20 mg (blue cap, white body); 30 mg (reddish brown cap, white body); 40 mg (yellow cap, white body); 60 mg (white cap, white body). Capsules are imprinted with the letters *UCB* on the cap and the dosage strength on the body.

This fact sheet is not intended to cover all possible medication uses, directions, precautions, drug interactions, or adverse effects and is not a substitute for specific medical advice or to be used as a guide for prescribing.

From *Medication Fact Sheets: A Behavioral Medication Reference for Educators* (3rd ed.), © 2010 by D.E. Konopasek, Champaign IL: Research Press (800-519-2707, www.researchpress.com).

METHYLIN   (Methylphenidate hydrochloride)

Methylin is available in generic form.

What is it for?

Methylin is most often used as a treatment for attention-deficit/hyperactivity disorder (ADHD). It has also been used to treat narcolepsy (sudden onset of sleep).

What does it do?

Methylin is a central nervous system stimulant. It appears to activate the brain stem arousal system and has been shown to be useful in helping individuals improve behaviors commonly associated with ADHD, with effects such as these:

1. Improved motor activity
2. Decreased disruptiveness
3. Improved concentration
4. Improved fine motor coordination
5. More goal-directed behavior
6. Decreased distractibility
7. Improved voice modulation

NOTE

Methylin is a controlled substance under DEA Schedule II (high potential for abuse; see Appendix C). Pregnancy Risk Category C (risk cannot be ruled out; see Appendix B).

What are the side effects?

Individuals taking Methylin may experience a wide range of side effects, including the following:

1. Loss of appetite
2. Insomnia
3. Upset stomach
4. Headache/dizziness
5. Nervousness
6. Tachycardia

NOTES

► Sudden death has been reported in individuals taking stimulant medications who have structural heart defects or other serious heart conditions.

► Medical literature reports that stimulants may intensify the motor and/or vocal tics characteristic of Tourette's syndrome.

► Individuals taking stimulant medications should not take monoamine oxidase inhibitors (MAOIs) at the same time or within 14 days of discontinuing treatment with an MAOI.

► Methylin should not be used in individuals with glaucoma.

What are the dosages and forms?

The safety and effectiveness of Methylin in children under the age of 6 has not been established. Therefore, its use in younger children is not recommended. Methylin is rapidly absorbed, with peak effects occurring approximately 2 hours after ingestion (approximately 5 hours in Methylin ER). In adults, the typical dosage is 20–30 mg/day, given in divided doses. For children over the age of 6, the maximum daily dosage should not exceed 60 mg/day, given in divided doses.

► Tablet form (Mallinckrodt): 5 mg (round, white); 10 mg (round, white); 20 mg (round, white). Each tablet is embossed with the dosage strength on one side and an *M* on the other. Methylin is also available in an extended release form as Methylin ER: 10 mg (round, white); 20 mg (round, white).

► Chewable tablet form (Mallinckrodt): 2.5 mg (square, white); 5 mg (square, white); 10 mg (square, white). Each grape-flavored tablet is embossed with *CHEW* and the dosage strength.

This fact sheet is not intended to cover all possible medication uses, directions, precautions, drug interactions, or adverse effects and is not a substitute for specific medical advice or to be used as a guide for prescribing.

From *Medication Fact Sheets: A Behavioral Medication Reference for Educators* (3rd ed.), © 2010 by D.E. Konopasek, Champaign IL: Research Press (800-519-2707, www.researchpress.com).

What is it for?

Moban is an antipsychotic medication used in the treatment of psychotic disorders.

What does it do?

Pharmacologically, Moban acts to block the effects of dopamine, a central nervous system neurotransmitter. It has the effect of reducing psychotic symptoms associated with schizophrenia (hallucinations and/or delusions).

NOTE

Pregnancy Risk Category C (risk cannot be ruled out; see Appendix B).

What are the side effects?

Individuals taking Moban may experience a wide range of side effects, including these:

1. Drowsiness/fatigue
2. Agitation/restlessness
3. Tremors
4. Muscle spasms
5. Dry mouth/blurred vision
6. Tardive dyskinesia/NMS

NOTES

► Tardive dyskinesia is a condition that may develop in individuals of any age group treated with antipsychotic medications for an extended period of time. Symptoms include involuntary movements of the face, tongue, mouth, or jaw and, to a lesser degree, involuntary rhythmic movements of the extremities. There is no known treatment for this condition.

► The medical literature has also reported the occurrence of neuroleptic malignant syndrome (NMS) in individuals taking antipsychotic medication. NMS is a rare but potentially fatal medication reaction involving a range of symptoms, including muscle rigidity, disorientation, irregular pulse and blood pressure, and tachycardia.

► Elderly individuals with dementia-related psychosis are at increased risk of death if treated with antipsychotic drugs and should not take Moban.

What are the dosages and forms?

The use of Moban in children under the age of 12 is not recommended due to a lack of clinical research studying its effectiveness in younger children. In adults, a therapeutic maintenance dosage range for moderately impaired individuals of 30–100 mg/day is not uncommon. Peak blood levels are reached approximately 1.5 hours after ingestion, and the effects last about 24–36 hours.

► Tablet form (Endo): 5 mg (round, orange); 10 mg (round, lavender); 25 mg (round, light green); 50 mg (round, blue). Tablets are imprinted with the word *MOBAN* along with the dosage strength.

This fact sheet is not intended to cover all possible medication uses, directions, precautions, drug interactions, or adverse effects and is not a substitute for specific medical advice or to be used as a guide for prescribing.

Mysoline is available in generic form.

What is it for?

Mysoline is an anticonvulsant medication and is used in the treatment of grand mal, psychomotor, and focal seizures.

What does it do?

Although the exact mechanism is unclear, Mysoline seems to raise the seizure threshold and alters seizure patterns, with the effect of decreasing or eliminating seizure activity.

NOTE

Pregnancy Risk Category D (positive evidence of risk; see Appendix B).

What are the side effects?

Individuals taking Mysoline may experience a wide range of side effects, including these:

1. Poor coordination
2. Dizziness
3. Nausea/vomiting
4. Fatigue
5. Decreased appetite
6. Irritability

NOTE

Antiseizure drugs should not be discontinued abruptly due to a risk of increased seizure activity.

What are the dosages and forms?

For children under the age of 8, the typical maintenance dosage of Mysoline is approximately 375–750 mg/day, given in three divided doses. For adults and children over the age of 8, the usual dosage is 750–1250 mg/day, given in three to four divided doses. Dosages above 2000 mg/day are not recommended.

► Tablet form (Valeant): 50 mg (square, white); 250 mg (square, yellow). Each tablet is imprinted with the word *MYSOLINE* and the dosage strength.

► Liquid form: Mysoline is available as a liquid suspension (250 mg/5 mL).

From *Medication Fact Sheets: A Behavioral Medication Reference for Educators* (3rd ed.), © 2010 by D.E. Konopasek, Champaign IL: Research Press (800-519-2707, www.researchpress.com).

What is it for?

Nardil is used in the treatment of major depressive disorder (MDD). Nardil is rarely used as the first antidepressant of choice but may be prescribed for individuals who do not respond to other types of antidepressants or who have an atypical depression.

What does it do?

Nardil belongs to a group of antidepressants known as monoamine oxidase inhibitors (MAOIs). Pharmacologically, Nardil seems to interfere with the reuptake of the neurotransmitters serotonin and norepinephrine by inhibiting the action of enzymes that normally break down these neurotransmitters. It has the effect of decreasing depressive symptoms.

NOTE

Pregnancy Risk Category C (risk cannot be ruled out; see Appendix B).

What are the side effects?

Individuals taking Nardil may experience a wide range of side effects, including these:

1. Sedation
2. Overactivity
3. Muscle cramps
4. Dizziness
5. Urinary hesitancy
6. Hypertensive crisis

NOTES

► Hypertensive crisis can be fatal. Nardil, along with other MAOIs, requires strict dietary vigilance. Individuals taking Nardil should take great care to avoid certain foods and beverages, such as beer, red wine, aged cheeses, dry sausage, fava or Italian green beans, brewers' yeast, smoked fish, and liver. This list of food products to be avoided is by no means exhaustive.

► Also, it is very important for individuals taking Nardil or other MAOIs not to take other medications without first checking with their physician. Demerol, epinephrine, local anesthetics, many antidepressants, and decongestants may be especially dangerous.

► Individuals taking Nardil should be monitored closely for the potential of worsening depression or the emergence of suicidal thoughts or behavior, particularly in the early stages of medication treatment or when dosages change.

What are the dosages and forms?

The use of Nardil in children under the age of 16 is not recommended due to the lack of studies demonstrating its effectiveness and safety. The maximum adult dose of Nardil is approximately 60–90 mg/day, usually given in divided doses. Maintenance dosages may be as low as 15 mg/day or every other day. Nardil is fairly rapidly absorbed, reaching peak plasma concentrations within an hour of ingestion.

► Tablet form (Pfizer): 15 mg (round, orange).

This fact sheet is not intended to cover all possible medication uses, directions, precautions, drug interactions, or adverse effects and is not a substitute for specific medical advice or to be used as a guide for prescribing.

NAVANE   (Thiothixene hydrochloride)

Navane is available in generic form.

What is it for?

Navane is an antipsychotic medication used in the treatment of psychotic disorders such as schizophrenia.

What does it do?

Pharmacologically, Navane acts to block the effects of dopamine, a central nervous system neurotransmitter. Navane improves cognitive functioning and reduces psychotic symptoms, including the delusions and hallucinations associated with schizophrenia.

NOTE

Pregnancy Risk Category C (risk cannot be ruled out; see Appendix B).

What are the side effects?

Individuals taking Navane may experience a wide range of side effects, including these:

1. Tremors/shakiness
2. Dry mouth
3. Blurred vision
4. Tardive dyskinesia/NMS
5. Lightheadedness
6. Restlessness
7. Dystonic reaction (extreme muscle spasms)

NOTES

► Tardive dyskinesia is a condition that may develop in individuals of any age group treated with antipsychotic medications for an extended period of time. Symptoms include involuntary movements of the face, tongue, mouth, or jaw and, to a lesser degree, involuntary rhythmic movements of the extremities. There is no known treatment for this condition.

► The medical literature has also reported the occurrence of neuroleptic malignant syndrome (NMS) in individuals taking antipsychotic medication.

NMS is a rare but potentially fatal medication reaction involving a range of symptoms, including muscle rigidity, disorientation, irregular pulse and blood pressure, and tachycardia.

► Elderly individuals with dementia-related psychosis are at increased risk of death if treated with antipsychotic drugs and should not take Navane.

What are the dosages and forms?

For children under the age of 12, the use of Navane is not recommended. The typical adult dosage is from 20–30 mg/day, although higher doses may be prescribed for more severe symptoms. Doses may be divided and taken two to three times daily.

► Capsule form (Pfizer): 1 mg (orange cap, yellow body); 2 mg (blue cap, yellow body); 5 mg (orange cap, white body); 10 mg (blue cap, white body); 20 mg (dark blue cap, light green body).

► Injection form (Pfizer): Navane is also available as an intramuscular injection (5 mg/mL).

From *Medication Fact Sheets: A Behavioral Medication Reference for Educators* (3rd ed.), © 2010 by D.E. Konopasek, Champaign IL: Research Press (800-519-2707, www.researchpress.com).

Serzone is now available only as generic nefazodone hydrochloride.

What is it for?

Nefazodone is an antidepressant and is used in the treatment of major depressive disorder (MDD).

What does it do?

Nefazodone relieves depressive symptoms, including anxiety and sleep disturbances associated with some forms of depression. Pharmacologically, nefazodone appears to inhibit the reuptake of the central nervous system neurotransmitters serotonin and norepinephrine.

NOTE

Pregnancy Risk Category C (risk cannot be ruled out; see Appendix B).

What are the side effects?

Individuals taking nefazodone may experience a wide range of side effects, including these:

1. Headache
2. Dry mouth
3. Nausea
4. Dizziness when standing up
5. Blurred vision
6. Liver failure

NOTES

► Cases of life-threatening liver failure have occurred in patients treated with nefazodone.

► It is recommended that nefazodone not be taken in combination with monoamine oxidase inhibitors (MAOIs) or within 14 days of discontinuing treatment with an MAOI. At least 7 days should be allowed after stopping nefazodone before starting an MAOI.

► Individuals taking nefazodone should be monitored closely for the potential of worsening depression or the emergence of suicidal thoughts or behavior, particularly in the early stages of medication treatment or when dosages change.

What are the dosages and forms?

The safety of nefazodone in children under the age of 18 has not been established. The effective dosage range for nefazodone is 300–600 mg/day, generally given in two doses. Nefazodone is rapidly absorbed in the body, with peak concentrations occurring within approximately an hour after ingestion. It may take several days for the therapeutic effect of nefazodone to become apparent.

► Tablet form (various pharmaceutical companies): 50 mg; 100 mg; 150 mg; 200 mg; 250 mg.

This fact sheet is not intended to cover all possible medication uses, directions, precautions, drug interactions, or adverse effects and is not a substitute for specific medical advice or to be used as a guide for prescribing.

From *Medication Fact Sheets: A Behavioral Medication Reference for Educators* (3rd ed.), © 2010 by D.E. Konopasek, Champaign IL: Research Press (800-519-2707, www.researchpress.com).

Neurontin is available in generic form.

What is it for?

Neurontin is an anticonvulsant medication used in the treatment of partial seizure disorders. It is generally used in conjunction with other antiseizure medications.

What does it do?

The mechanism by which Neurontin exhibits an antiseizure effect is unclear. It appears to activate gamma-aminobutyric acid (GABA), which is a neurotransmitter involved in inhibiting seizure activity.

NOTE

Pregnancy Risk Category C (risk cannot be ruled out; see Appendix B).

What are the side effects?

Individuals taking Neurontin may experience a wide range of side effects, including these:

1. Headache
2. Fatigue/drowsiness
3. Dizziness
4. Blurred vision
5. Tremors
6. Anxiety/irritability

NOTES

- ► Antiseizure drugs should not be discontinued abruptly due to a risk of increased seizure activity.

- ► The use of Neurontin to treat epilepsy in children ages 3–11 has been associated with adverse central nervous system symptoms such as agitation, aggression, thought disorder, and restlessness.

What are the dosages and forms?

The typical adult dosage is 900–1800 mg/day, given in divided doses (usually three times per day). In children 5 years of age and older, the usual daily dose is 25–35 mg/kg/day, given in three doses. For children ages 3–4, the typical daily dosage is 40 mg/kg/day, given in three doses. Peak plasma levels occur 2–3 hours after ingestion.

- ► Capsule form (Pfizer): 100 mg (white cap, white body); 300 mg (yellow cap, yellow body); 400 mg (orange cap, orange body). The word *NEURONTIN* is printed on each capsule, along with the dosage strength.

- ► Tablet form (Pfizer): 600 mg (elliptical, white); 800 mg (elliptical, white). Tablets are imprinted with *NT* along with the dosage strength.

- ► Liquid form (Pfizer): Neurontin is available as an oral solution (250 mg/5 mL).

This fact sheet is not intended to cover all possible medication uses, directions, precautions, drug interactions, or adverse effects and is not a substitute for specific medical advice or to be used as a guide for prescribing.

From *Medication Fact Sheets: A Behavioral Medication Reference for Educators* (3rd ed.), © 2010 by D.E. Konopasek, Champaign IL: Research Press (800-519-2707, www.researchpress.com).

Norpramin is available in generic form.

What is it for?

Norpramin is a tricyclic antidepressant and is used in the treatment of major depressive disorder (MDD).

What does it do?

Norpramin has the effect of elevating mood and improving cognitive functioning, psychomotor functioning, and concentration. Pharmacologically, Norpramin appears to inhibit the reuptake of norepinephrine and serotonin, central nervous system neurotransmitters.

NOTE

Pregnancy Risk Category C (risk cannot be ruled out; see Appendix B).

What are the side effects?

Individuals taking Norpramin may experience a wide range of side effects, including these:

1. Blood pressure changes
2. Dry mouth/blurred vision
3. Nausea/gastric distress
4. Restlessness/agitation
5. Weight change
6. Perspiration/flushing

NOTE

► It is recommended that Norpramin not be taken in combination with monoamine oxidase inhibitors (MAOIs) or within 14 days of discontinuing treatment with an MAOI. At least 14 days should be allowed after stopping Norpramin before starting an MAOI.

► Individuals taking Norpramin should be monitored closely for the potential of worsening depression or the emergence of suicidal thoughts or behavior, particularly in the early stages of medication treatment or when dosages change.

What are the dosages and forms?

Norpramin is not recommended for younger children due to a lack of research as to its effectiveness and safety with this age group. The usual adolescent dose is 25–100 mg/day. Doses may be given singly or divided. The typical adult dose is 100–200 mg/day. Norpramin is rapidly absorbed in the body, although it may take 2–3 weeks for the full therapeutic effect to be observed.

► Tablet form (Sanofi-Aventis): 10 mg (round, blue); 25 mg (round, yellow); 50 mg (round, green); 75 mg (round, orange); 100 mg (round, peach); 150 mg (round, white). Tablets are imprinted with the word *NORPRAMIN* along with the dosage strength.

What is it for?

Orap is an antipsychotic medication but is most often used to treat motor and vocal tics associated with Tourette's syndrome in individuals who fail to respond to more standard treatments. It is not intended as a treatment of first choice.

What does it do?

Pharmacologically, Orap acts to block the action of dopamine, a central nervous system neurotransmitter. The effect is to reduce both motor and vocal involuntary tics.

NOTE

Pregnancy Risk Category C (risk cannot be ruled out; see Appendix B).

What are the side effects?

Individuals taking Orap may experience a wide range of side effects, including these:

1. Changes in heart rhythms
2. Dry mouth/blurred vision
3. Nausea/vomiting
4. Agitation/restlessness
5. Sedation
6. Tardive dyskinesia/NMS

NOTES

► Tardive dyskinesia is a condition that may develop in individuals of any age group treated with antipsychotic medications for an extended period of time. Symptoms include involuntary movements of the face, tongue, mouth, or jaw and, to a lesser degree, involuntary rhythmic movements of the extremities. There is no known treatment for this condition.

► The medical literature has also reported the occurrence of neuroleptic malignant syndrome (NMS) in individuals taking antipsychotic medication. NMS is a rare but potentially fatal medication reaction involving a range of symptoms, including muscle rigidity, disorientation, irregular pulse and blood pressure, and tachycardia.

► Orap is not recommended in individuals with cardiac arrhythmias.

► Individuals taking Orap should avoid drinking grapefruit juice.

► Elderly individuals with dementia-related psychosis are at increased risk of death if treated with antipsychotic drugs and should not take Orap.

What are the dosages and forms?

There is very little information related to the use of Orap in children under 12 years of age except for treating Tourette's syndrome. Therefore, its use with younger children for any other purpose is not recommended. In adults, dosages greater than 10 mg/day (or 0.2 mg/kg/day, whichever is less) are not recommended. Peak blood levels occur 6–8 hours after administration and maintain a therapeutic level for approximately 50–60 hours.

► Tablet form (Gate): 1 mg (oval, white); 2 mg (oval, white). Tablets are imprinted with the word *LEMMON* on one side and *ORAP* on the other.

This fact sheet is not intended to cover all possible medication uses, directions, precautions, drug interactions, or adverse effects and is not a substitute for specific medical advice or to be used as a guide for prescribing.

Oxazepam is available only in generic form.

What is it for?

Oxazepam in an antianxiety medication typically used as a short-term treatment for anxiety disorders. It has been found to be particularly useful in treating anxiety and tension associated with depression as well as in managing anxiety in older individuals. It is also used in treating alcohol withdrawal symptoms (tremors, anxiety, etc.).

What does it do?

Oxazepam is a central nervous system depressant and exerts a calming effect. It appears to block the arousal of certain higher functioning brain centers. Oxazepam belongs to the drug class benzodiazepine. Long-term use is not recommended.

NOTE

Oxazepam is a controlled substance under DEA Schedule IV (see Appendix C). Pregnancy Risk Category D (positive evidence of risk; see Appendix B).

What are the side effects?

Individuals taking oxazepam may experience a wide range of side effects, including these:

1. Drowsiness
2. Decreased blood pressure
3. Dizziness
4. Nausea
5. Headache
6. Skin rash

NOTE

Withdrawal symptoms (cramping, vomiting, convulsions, sweating, etc.) have been reported following abrupt discontinuation of oxazepam. Individuals who are prone to substance abuse/addiction should be monitored carefully when taking oxazepam due to the possibility for psychological and physiological dependence.

What are the dosages and forms?

After ingestion, oxazepam reaches peak plasma levels in approximately 3 hours, maintaining a therapeutic effect for 6–10 hours. Oxazepam is not recommended for children under 6 years of age. The typical adult dose is 15–30 mg, given three to four times per day.

► Capsule form (Sandoz): 10 mg (white cap, white body); 15 mg (white cap, white body); 30 mg (white cap, white body). Capsules are imprinted with *GG* on cap and body.

This fact sheet is not intended to cover all possible medication uses, directions, precautions, drug interactions, or adverse effects and is not a substitute for specific medical advice or to be used as a guide for prescribing.

From *Medication Fact Sheets: A Behavioral Medication Reference for Educators* (3rd ed.), © 2010 by D.E. Konopasek, Champaign IL: Research Press (800-519-2707, www.researchpress.com).

Pamelor is available in generic form. AVENTYL and SENSIVAL are other brand names for nortriptyline hydrochloride.

What is it for?

Pamelor is a tricyclic antidepressant used in the treatment of major depressive disorder (MDD).

What does it do?

Pamelor has the effect of elevating mood, relieving the tension and anxiety associated with depression, improving cognitive functioning, and increasing concentration. Pharmacologically, Pamelor appears to increase the availability of norepinephrine and serotonin.

NOTE

Pregnancy Risk Category C (risk cannot be ruled out, see Appendix B).

What are the side effects?

Individuals taking Pamelor may experience a wide range of side effects, including these:

1. Drowsiness
2. Urinary retention
3. Dizziness
4. Dry mouth/blurred vision
5. Weight gain
6. Sweating/chills/flushing

NOTES

► It is recommended that Pamelor not be taken in combination with monoamine oxidase inhibitors (MAOIs) or within 14 days of discontinuing treatment with an MAOI. At least 14 days should be allowed after stopping Pamelor before starting an MAOI.

► Individuals with cardiovascular disease who take Pamelor should be monitored closely due to the risk of developing potentially serious cardiac irregularities.

► Individuals taking Pamelor should be monitored closely for the potential of worsening depression or the emergence of suicidal thoughts or behavior, particularly in the early stages of medication treatment or when dosages change.

What are the dosages and forms?

Pamelor is not recommended for children under 12 years of age due to a lack of research demonstrating its effectiveness and safety with this age group. The usual adolescent dose is 30–50 mg/day, given either singly or in divided doses. The usual adult dose is 75–100 mg/day, given in divided doses. Doses above 150 mg/day are not recommended.

► Capsule form (Mallinckrodt): 10 mg (orange cap, white body); 25 mg (orange cap, white body); 50 mg (white cap, white body); 75 mg (orange cap, orange body). Capsules are imprinted with the word *PAMELOR* and the dosage strength.

► Liquid form (Mallinckrodt): Pamelor is available in solution form (10 mg/5 mL).

This fact sheet is not intended to cover all possible medication uses, directions, precautions, drug interactions, or adverse effects and is not a substitute for specific medical advice or to be used as a guide for prescribing.

From *Medication Fact Sheets: A Behavioral Medication Reference for Educators* (3rd ed.), © 2010 by D.E. Konopasek, Champaign IL: Research Press (800-519-2707, www.researchpress.com).

Parnate is available in generic form.

What is it for?

Parnate is used in the treatment of major depressive disorder (MDD). It is usually only used in individuals who do not respond to other types of antidepressants.

What does it do?

Parnate belongs to a group of antidepressants known as monoamine oxidase inhibitors (MAOIs). Pharmacologically, Parnate seems to increase the concentration of the neurotransmitters epinephrine, norepinephrine, and serotonin within storage sites in brain cells. This has the effect of decreasing depressive symptoms.

NOTE

Pregnancy Risk Category C (risk cannot be ruled out; see Appendix B).

What are the side effects?

Individuals taking Parnate may experience a wide range of side effects, including these:

1. Drowsiness
2. Overactivity
3. Abdominal pain
4. Dizziness
5. Headache
6. Hypertensive crisis

NOTES

Hypertensive crisis can be fatal.

► Parnate, along with other MAOIs, requires strict dietary vigilance. Individuals taking Parnate should take great care to avoid certain foods and beverages, such as beer, red wine, aged cheeses, dry sausage, fava or Italian green beans, brewers' yeast, smoked fish, and liver. This list of food products to be avoided is by no means exhaustive.

► It is very important for individuals taking Parnate or other MAOIs not to take other medications without first checking with their physician. Many antidepressants, epinephrine, local anesthetics, and decongestants may be especially dangerous in combination with Parnate.

► Parnate is not recommended for individuals with either cerebrovascular defects or cardiovascular disorders.

► Individuals taking Parnate should be monitored closely for the potential of worsening depression or the emergence of suicidal thoughts or behavior, particularly in the early stages of medication treatment or when dosages change.

What are the dosages and forms?

The effective adult dose of Parnate is approximately 30 mg/day, usually given in divided doses. A therapeutic response to Parnate may occur in 1–3 weeks.

► Tablet form (GlaxoSmithKline): 10 mg (round, peach). Each tablet is imprinted with the word *PARNATE.*

Paxil is available in generic form. PEXEVA is the trade name for Paroxetine mesylate, an alternate chemical form of Paxil.

What is it for?

Paxil is an antidepressant and is used in the treatment of major depressive disorder (MDD). It is also often used to treat obsessive-compulsive disorder (OCD), panic attacks, post traumatic stress disorder (PTSD), generalized anxiety disorder (GAD), and social anxiety disorder.

What does it do?

Paxil belongs to a group of antidepressants known as selective serotonin reuptake inhibitors (SSRIs). As such, it acts to block or inhibit the reabsorption of serotonin, a central nervous system neurotransmitter. The intended effect is elevation of mood, improved cognitive and psychomotor functioning, and improved concentration.

NOTE

Pregnancy Risk Category D (positive evidence of risk; see Appendix B).

What are the side effects?

Individuals taking Paxil may experience a wide range of side effects, including these:

1. Stomach upset/nausea
2. Insomnia/agitation
3. Dizziness
4. Headache
5. Blurred vision
6. Dry mouth

NOTES

- ► It is recommended that Paxil not be taken in combination with monoamine oxidase inhibitors (MAOIs) or within 14 days of discontinuing treatment with an MAOI. At least 14 days should be allowed after stopping Paxil before starting an MAOI.

- ► A serious, potentially life-threatening condition known as serotonin syndrome can occur when SSRIs and certain medications used to treat migraine headaches (triptans) are taken together.

- ► Paxil should not be taken in combination with thioridazine (Mellaril) due to the potential for serious cardiac irregularities.

- ► Paxil should not be discontinued abruptly. Gradual discontinuation should occur under medical supervision.

- ► Individuals taking Paxil should be monitored closely for the potential of worsening depression or the emergence of suicidal thoughts or behavior, particularly in the early stages of medication treatment or when dosages change.

What are the dosages and forms?

The safety and effectiveness of Paxil for use with children has not been established. A common adult dosage for Paxil is 20–50 mg/day, given in a single morning dose. Full therapeutic effect may take 10 days to be observed.

- ► Tablet form (GlaxoSmithKline): 10 mg (oval, yellow); 20 mg (oval, pink); 30 mg (oval, blue); 40 mg (oval, green). Tablets have the word PAXIL imprinted on one side and the dosage strength on the other. PEXEVA (Noven) is available in the following strengths: 10 mg (oval, white); 20 mg (oval, dark orange); 30 mg (oval, yellow); 40 mg (oval, rose).

- ► Controlled release form (GlaxoSmithKline): Paxil is available in controlled release form as Paxil CR, 12.5 mg (round, yellow); 25 mg (round, pink); 37.5 mg (round, blue). Tablets are imprinted with PAXIL CR along with the dosage strength.

- ► Liquid form (GlaxoSmithKline): Paxil is available as a liquid suspension (10 mg/5 mL).

This fact sheet is not intended to cover all possible medication uses, directions, precautions, drug interactions, or adverse effects and is not a substitute for specific medical advice or to be used as a guide for prescribing.

Trilafon is now available only as generic perphenazine.

What is it for?

Perphenazine is used in the management of psychotic disorders as well as in the treatment of severe nausea and vomiting, hiccups, and anxiety.

What does it do?

Perphenazine is an antipsychotic drug with a mild sedating effect. It helps reduce psychotic symptoms (hallucinations and/or delusions). Pharmacologically, it is presumed that perphenazine acts to block the action of dopamine, a central nervous system neurotransmitter.

NOTE

Pregnancy Risk Category C (risk cannot be ruled out; see Appendix B).

What are the side effects?

Individuals taking perphenazine may experience a wide range of side effects, including these:

1. Mild sedation/fatigue
2. Agitation/restlessness
3. Muscle spasms
4. Hypotension/dizziness
5. Dry mouth/blurred vision
6. Tardive dyskinesia/NMS

NOTES

► Tardive dyskinesia is a condition that may develop in individuals of any age group treated with antipsychotic medications for an extended period of time. Symptoms include involuntary movements of the face, tongue, mouth, or jaw and, to a lesser degree, involuntary rhythmic movements of the extremities. There is no known treatment for this condition.

► The medical literature has also reported the occurrence of neuroleptic malignant syndrome (NMS) in individuals taking antipsychotic medication. NMS is a rare but potentially fatal medication reaction involving a range of symptoms, including muscle rigidity, disorientation, irregular pulse and blood pressure, and tachycardia.

► Elderly individuals with dementia-related psychosis are at increased risk of death if treated with antipsychotic drugs and should not take perphenazine.

What are the dosages and forms?

Doses for children under the age of 12 have not yet been established. Children over the age of 12 may receive a low adult dosage (4–12 mg/day). The typical adult dosage is 8–24 mg/day. Prolonged dosage above 64 mg/day is not recommended. Perphenazine enters the bloodstream fairly rapidly, reaching a peak plasma level in 1–3 hours with steady state concentrations occurring approximately 72 hours after ingestion.

► Tablet form (various pharmaceutical companies): 2 mg; 4 mg; 8 mg; 16 mg.

► Liquid form: Perphenazine is available as an oral concentrate (16 mg/5 mL).

► Injection form: Perphenazine is available as an intramuscular injection (5 mg/mL).

Phenobarbital is available only in generic form.

What is it for?

Phenobarbital is a central nervous system depressant often used as a sedative and for the treatment of generalized and partial seizures. It has also been used as a treatment for anxiety disorders.

What does it do?

Phenobarbital is a barbiturate and depresses the sensory cortex of the brain and decreases motor activity, producing drowsiness and sedation.

NOTE

Phenobarbital is a controlled substance under DEA Schedule IV (see Appendix C). Pregnancy Risk Category D (positive evidence of risk; see Appendix B).

What are the side effects?

Individuals taking phenobarbital may experience a wide range of side effects, including these:

1. Drowsiness/lethargy

2. Nausea

3. Headache

4. Dizziness

5. Restlessness

6. Irritability and hyperactivity (especially in children)

What are the dosages and forms?

As an anticonvulsant, the usual dosage for children is 3–6 mg/kg/day. (e.g., for a 70-pound child, this equates to 95–190 mg/day). For adults, the dosage range is typically 60–200 mg/day. Phenobarbital is a long-acting barbiturate. It reaches peak blood levels in about an hour after ingestion and has a duration of action of 10–12 hours.

► Forms of administration: Phenobarbital is available in a variety of forms (tablets, capsules, elixir, sustained action capsules, injection) by various pharmaceutical companies. Therefore, a description of each form of administration (dose, shape, color) is not practical for this format.

From *Medication Fact Sheets: A Behavioral Medication Reference for Educators* (3rd ed.), © 2010 by D.E. Konopasek, Champaign IL: Research Press (800-519-2707, www.researchpress.com).

What is it for?

Pristiq is an antidepressant and is used for the treatment of major depressive disorder (MDD).

What does it do?

Pristiq is a selective serotonin and norepinephrine reuptake inhibitor (SSNRI). It appears to increase the availability and activity of the neurotransmitters serotonin and norepinephrine. The intended effect is an elevation of mood, improved cognitive and psychomotor functioning, and improved concentration.

NOTE

Pregnancy Risk Category C (risk cannot be ruled out; see Appendix B).

What are the side effects?

Individuals taking Pristiq may experience a wide range of side effects, including these:

1. Nausea
2. Elevated blood pressure
3. Diarrhea/constipation
4. Decreased appetite
5. Fatigue/sleepiness
6. Dizziness/nervousness

NOTES

- A serious, potentially life-threatening condition known as serotonin syndrome can occur when SSRIs and certain medications used to treat migraine headaches (triptans) are taken together.

- It is recommended that Pristiq not be taken in combination with monoamine oxidase inhibitors (MAOIs) or within 14 days of discontinuing treatment with an MAOI. At least 14 days should be allowed after stopping Pristiq before starting an MAOI.

- Individuals taking Pristiq should be monitored closely for the potential of worsening depression or the emergence of suicidal thoughts or behavior, particularly in the early stages of medication treatment or when dosages change.

- Individuals with narrow-angle glaucoma should be monitored closely while taking Pristiq.

What are the dosages and forms?

The safety and effectiveness of Pristiq in children has not been established. The typical adult dose for Pristiq is 50 mg, given once daily. Steady state concentrations of Pristiq occur within 4–5 days.

- Extended release tablet form (Wyeth): 50 mg (square, pink); 100 mg (square, reddish orange). Tablets are marked with a *W* and the dosage strength.

This fact sheet is not intended to cover all possible medication uses, directions, precautions, drug interactions, or adverse effects and is not a substitute for specific medical advice or to be used as a guide for prescribing.

Prochlorperazine is available only in generic form.

What is it for?

Prochlorperazine is an antipsychotic medication used in the management of psychotic disorders. It is also used to control severe nausea and vomiting.

What does it do?

Prochlorperazine seems to block the action of dopamine, a central nervous system neurotransmitter. It is a moderately sedating drug and helps to reduce psychotic symptoms (hallucinations and/or delusions). It also has the effect of blocking or reducing the stimulation of vomiting.

NOTE

Pregnancy Risk Category C (risk cannot be ruled out; see Appendix B).

What are the side effects?

Individuals taking prochlorperazine may experience a wide range of side effects, including these:

1. Sedation/fatigue
2. Agitation/restlessness
3. Tremors/shakiness
4. Dizziness when standing up
5. Dry mouth/blurred vision
6. Tardive dyskinesia/NMS

NOTES

► Tardive dyskinesia is a condition that may develop in individuals of any age group treated with antipsychotic medications for an extended period of time. Symptoms include involuntary movements of the face, tongue, mouth, or jaw and, to a lesser degree, involuntary rhythmic movements of the extremities. There is no known treatment for this condition.

► The medical literature has also reported the occurrence of neuroleptic malignant syndrome (NMS) in individuals taking antipsychotic medication. NMS is a rare but potentially fatal medication reaction involving a range of symptoms, including muscle rigidity, disorientation, irregular pulse and blood pressure, and tachycardia.

► Prochlorperazine should be used only under close medical supervision with children experiencing acute illnesses, such as chicken pox or measles, or showing symptoms of Reye's syndrome.

What are the dosages and forms?

Prochlorperazine is not recommended for children under 20 pounds or under 2 years of age. For children 20–29 pounds, the usual dosage is 2–5 mg/day. For children 30–39 pounds, the usual dosage is 2.5–7.5 mg/day. For children 40–85 pounds, the typical dosage is 7.5–10 mg/day. For adult treatment of psychotic disorders, the dosage may range from 15–40 mg/day, usually given in divided doses.

► Tablet form (various pharmaceutical companies): 5 mg; 10 mg.

► Time-release capsule form (various pharmaceutical companies): 10 mg; 15 mg.

► Other forms: Prochlorperazine is also available in the form of suppositories, syrup, vial, and intramuscular injection.

This fact sheet is not intended to cover all possible medication uses, directions, precautions, drug interactions, or adverse effects and is not a substitute for specific medical advice or to be used as a guide for prescribing.

From *Medication Fact Sheets: A Behavioral Medication Reference for Educators* (3rd ed.), © 2010 by D.E. Konopasek, Champaign IL: Research Press (800-519-2707, www.researchpress.com).

Prozac is available in generic form. SARAFEM is another trade name for fluoxetine.

What is it for?

Prozac is an antidepressant and is used in the treatment of major depressive disorder (MDD). It has also been used in the treatment of panic attacks, obsessive-compulsive disorder (OCD), and bulimia. It is marketed for premenstrual dysphoric disorder (PMDD) under the trade name Sarafem.

What does it do?

Prozac belongs to a group of antidepressants known as selective serotonin reuptake inhibitors (SSRIs). As such, it acts to block or inhibit the reabsorption of serotonin, a central nervous system neurotransmitter. The intended effect is elevation of mood, improved cognitive and psychomotor functioning, and improved concentration.

NOTE

Pregnancy Risk Category C (risk cannot be ruled out; see Appendix B).

What are the side effects?

Individuals taking Prozac may experience a wide range of side effects, including these:

1. Nausea
2. Dizziness/lightheadedness
3. Headache/drowsiness
4. Tremor/shakiness
5. Sweating
6. Dry mouth

NOTES

► A serious, potentially life-threatening condition known as serotonin syndrome can occur when SSRIs and certain medications used to treat migraine headaches (triptans) are taken together.

► It is recommended that Prozac not be taken in combination with monoamine oxidase inhibitors (MAOIs) or within 14 days of discontinuing treatment with an MAOI. At least 14 days should be allowed after stopping Prozac before starting an MAOI.

► Prozac should not be taken in combination with thioridazine (Mellaril) or within 5 weeks after Prozac has been discontinued due to the potential for serious cardiac irregularities.

► Individuals taking Prozac should be monitored closely for the potential of worsening depression or the emergence of suicidal thoughts or behavior, particularly in the early stages of medication treatment or when dosages change.

What are the dosages and forms?

The recommended adult dose for treating depression and OCD is 20–80 mg/day, given in one to two doses, or 10–20 mg/day for children and adolescents. For bulimia, the recommended adult dose is 60 mg/day, given in the morning. The maximum dose is 80 mg/day. Peak blood levels occur within 6–8 hours. It may take up to 4–5 weeks for the full antidepressant effect of Prozac to be observed.

► Capsule form (Pulvules) (Eli Lilly): 10 mg (green cap, green body); 20 mg (light green cap, yellow body); 40 mg (green cap, orange body). Prozac is also available in time-release form as Prozac Weekly: 90 mg (green cap, clear body).

► Tablet form (various pharmaceutical companies): 10 mg; 20 mg; 40 mg.

► Liquid form (various pharmaceutical companies): Prozac is available as an oral solution (20 mg/5 mL).

This fact sheet is not intended to cover all possible medication uses, directions, precautions, drug interactions, or adverse effects and is not a substitute for specific medical advice or to be used as a guide for prescribing.

From *Medication Fact Sheets: A Behavioral Medication Reference for Educators* (3rd ed.), © 2010 by D.E. Konopasek, Champaign IL: Research Press (800-519-2707, www.researchpress.com).

What is it for?

Remeron is an antidepressant and is used in the treatment of major depressive disorder (MDD).

What does it do?

Remeron has the main effect of elevating mood, improving cognitive and psychomotor functioning, and increasing concentration. Pharmacologically, Remeron acts to stimulate the release and availability of the neurotransmitters norepinephrine and serotonin and to block specific serotonin receptor sites.

NOTE

Pregnancy Risk Category C (risk cannot be ruled out; see Appendix B).

What are the side effects?

Individuals taking Remeron may experience a wide range of side effects, including these:

1. Drowsiness

2. Increased appetite

3. Increased appetite/weight gain

4. Dizziness

5. Dry mouth

6. Upset stomach

7. Agranulocytosis

NOTES

► Agranulocytosis is a rare but serious blood disorder in which a person's white blood cell count drops precipitously, causing a serious risk of death because of lowered resistance to infection.

► It is recommended that Remeron not be taken in combination with monoamine oxidase inhibitors (MAOIs) or within 14 days of discontinuing treatment with an MAOI. At least 14 days should be allowed after stopping Remeron before starting an MAOI.

► Individuals taking Remeron should be monitored closely for the potential of worsening depression or the emergence of suicidal thoughts or behavior,

particularly in the early stages of medication treatment or when dosages change.

What are the dosages and forms?

The usual dosage for Remeron is 15–45 mg/day, given in a single bedtime dose. Remeron is rapidly absorbed and reaches peak blood levels approximately 2 hours after ingestion. As with many antidepressant medications, it may take several weeks for the full therapeutic effect of Remeron to become apparent.

► Tablet form (Organon): 15 mg (oval, yellow); 30 mg (oval, reddish brown); 45 mg (oval, white). Tablets are embossed with the word *Organon*. Remeron is also available in an orally disintegrating form as Remeron SolTab (Organon): 15 mg (round, white); 30 mg (round, white); 45 mg (round, white).

Restoril is available in generic form.

What is it for?

Restoril is used in the short-term (7–10 days) treatment of insomnia.

What does it do?

Restoril is a central nervous system depressant and appears to help induce sleep by blocking the arousal of certain higher functioning brain centers. Restoril belongs to the drug class benzodiazepine.

NOTE

Restoril is a controlled substance under DEA Schedule IV (see Appendix C). Pregnancy Risk Category X (contraindicated in pregnancy; see Appendix B).

What are the side effects?

Individuals taking Restoril may experience a wide variety of side effects, including these:

1. Drowsiness
2. Dizziness
3. Headache
4. Disorientation
5. Upset stomach
6. Impaired coordination

NOTE

Withdrawal symptoms (cramping, vomiting, convulsions, sweating, etc.) have been reported following abrupt discontinuation of Restoril. Individuals who are prone to substance abuse/addiction should be monitored carefully when taking Restoril due to the possibility for psychological and physiological dependence.

What are the dosages and forms?

The safety of Restoril in children under the age of 18 has not been established. The usual adult dose of Restoril is 15 mg/day, given before bedtime, although dosages may range from 7.5–30 mg/day. Restoril enters the bloodstream very quickly, with peak blood levels usually reached within 90 minutes.

► Capsule form (Mallinckrodt): 7.5 mg (blue cap, pink body); 15 mg (red cap, pink body); 22.5 mg (blue cap, blue body); 30 mg (red cap, blue body). Each cap is imprinted with the word *RESTORIL* and the dosage. Each body is imprinted with the words *FOR SLEEP.*

This fact sheet is not intended to cover all possible medication uses, directions, precautions, drug interactions, or adverse effects and is not a substitute for specific medical advice or to be used as a guide for prescribing.

From *Medication Fact Sheets: A Behavioral Medication Reference for Educators* (3rd ed.), © 2010 by D.E. Konopasek, Champaign IL: Research Press (800-519-2707, www.researchpress.com).

What is it for?

Risperdal is an antipsychotic drug used in the treatment of schizophrenia. It is also approved as a short-term treatment of acute manic or mixed episodes associated with bipolar disorder and as a treatment for irritability (aggression, self-injury, tantrums) associated with autistic disorder in children and adolescents ages 5–16 years.

What does it do?

Risperdal acts to improve cognitive functioning and mood as well as to reduce psychotic symptoms associated with schizophrenia (delusions and hallucinations). Pharmacologically, it appears Risperdal primarily blocks the effects of dopamine and serotonin, both central nervous system neurotransmitters.

NOTE

Pregnancy Risk Category C (risk cannot be ruled out; see Appendix B).

What are the side effects?

Individuals taking Risperdal may experience a wide range of side effects, including these:

1. Dizziness when standing up
2. Tremors/shakiness
3. Nausea
4. Anxiety
5. Constipation
6. Tardive dyskinesia/NMS

NOTES

▶ Tardive dyskinesia is a condition that may develop in individuals of any age group treated with antipsychotic medications for an extended period of time. Symptoms include involuntary movements of the face, tongue, mouth, or jaw and, to a lesser degree, involuntary rhythmic movements of the extremities. There is no known treatment for this condition.

▶ The medical literature has also reported the occurrence of neuroleptic malignant syndrome (NMS) in individuals taking antipsychotic medication. NMS is a rare but potentially fatal medication reaction involving a range of symptoms, including muscle rigidity, disorientation, irregular pulse and blood pressure, and tachycardia.

▶ There is a risk of stroke, particularly in elderly individuals being treated with Risperdal for dementia-related psychosis.

▶ Elderly individuals with dementia-related psychosis are at increased risk of death if treated with antipsychotic drugs and should not take Risperdal.

▶ There is a risk of developing hyperglycemia and diabetes mellitus in individuals treated with atypical antipsychotic medications, including Risperdal.

What are the dosages and forms?

For schizophrenia, the typical adult dosage of Risperdal is 4–8 mg/day, given in one or two doses. For adolescents with schizophrenia, the recommended daily dosage is 1–3 mg/day. Risperdal enters the bloodstream fairly quickly, with peak blood levels occurring approximately 3 hours after ingestion. It may take several days for the full therapeutic effects of Risperdal to become apparent.

▶ Tablet form (Janssen): 0.25 mg (capsule-shaped, dark yellow); 0.50 (capsule-shaped, reddish brown); 1 mg (capsule-shaped, white); 2 mg (capsule-shaped, orange); 3 mg (capsule-shaped, yellow); 4 mg (capsule-shaped, green). Tablets are imprinted with the word *JANSSEN* and *R* or *Ris* along with the dosage strength. Risperdal is also available in an orally disintegrating tablet form as Risperdal M-TAB: 0.5 mg (round, light coral); 1 mg (square, light coral); 2 mg (round, light coral).

▶ Liquid form (Janssen): Risperdal is available in solution form (1.0 mg/mL).

▶ Injection form (Janssen): Risperdal is available in a long-acting injection form as Risperdal Consta.

 From *Medication Fact Sheets: A Behavioral Medication Reference for Educators* (3rd ed.), © 2010 by D.E. Konopasek, Champaign IL: Research Press (800-519-2707, www.researchpress.com).

Ritalin is available in generic form.

What is it for?

Ritalin is most often used in the treatment of attention-deficit/hyperactivity disorder (ADHD). It has also been used as a treatment for narcolepsy (sudden, usually brief attacks of deep sleep).

What does it do?

Ritalin is a central nervous system stimulant. It appears to activate the brain stem arousal system. It has been shown to be useful in helping individuals improve behaviors commonly associated with ADHD, with effects such as these:

1. Improved motor activity
2. Decreased disruptiveness
3. Improved concentration
4. Improved fine motor coordination
5. More goal-directed behavior
6. Decreased distractibility
7. Improved voice modulation

NOTE

Ritalin is a controlled substance under DEA Schedule II (high potential for abuse; see Appendix C). Pregnancy Risk Category C (risk cannot be ruled out; see Appendix B).

What are the side effects?

Individuals taking Ritalin may experience a wide range of side effects, including the following:

1. Loss of appetite
2. Insomnia
3. Stomachache
4. Irritability and anxiety
5. Headache/dizziness
6. Tachycardia

NOTES

▶ Sudden death has been reported in individuals taking stimulant medications who have structural heart defects or other serious heart conditions.

▶ Medical literature reports that stimulants may intensify the motor and/or vocal tics characteristic of Tourette's syndrome.

▶ Individuals taking stimulant medications should not take monoamine oxidase inhibitors (MAOIs) at the same time or within 14 days of discontinuing treatment with an MAOI.

What are the dosages and forms?

Ritalin is not recommended for children under the age of 6. For children 6 years and older, the dosage may range from 5–60 mg/day.

▶ Tablet form (Novartis): 5 mg (round, yellow); 10 mg (round, pale green); 20 mg (round, pale yellow). This "fast acting" form typically reaches peak blood levels in just under 2 hours. Doses are often administered 2–3 times daily. All tablets are imprinted with the word *Ciba*.

▶ Sustained release (SR) tablet form (Novartis): 20 mg (round, white). Tablets are imprinted with the word *Ciba*. This form reaches peak blood level in approximately 4–5 hours and has a therapeutic effect for about 8 hours.

▶ Capsule form (Novartis): Ritalin is available in "once a day" extended release form as Ritalin LA, 10 mg (white cap, tan body); 20 mg (white cap and body); 30 mg (yellow cap and body); 40 mg (light brown cap and body). This form of methylphenidate has two distinct "peaks" occurring approximately four hours apart, with the first peak occurring approximately one hour after ingestion.

What is it for?

Seroquel is an atypical antipsychotic medication and is used in the treatment of schizophrenia. It is also approved as a treatment for acute manic episodes of bipolar disorder.

What does it do?

It is presumed that Seroquel's therapeutic effect is due primarily to its ability to block the effects of two central nervous system neurotransmitters, dopamine and serotonin. This has the effect of reducing the psychotic symptoms associated with schizophrenia (hallucinations and/or delusions) and acute manic behavior associated with bipolar disorder.

NOTE

Pregnancy Risk Category C (risk cannot be ruled out; see Appendix B).

What are the side effects?

Individuals taking Seroquel may experience a wide range of side effects, including these:

1. Drowsiness
2. Dizziness when standing up
3. Constipation
4. Irregular heartbeat
5. Weight gain
6. Tardive dyskinesia/NMS

NOTES

► Tardive dyskinesia is a condition that may develop in individuals of any age group treated with antipsychotic medications for an extended period of time. Symptoms include involuntary movements of the face, tongue, mouth, or jaw and, to a lesser degree, involuntary rhythmic movements of the extremities. There is no known treatment for this condition.

► The medical literature has also reported the occurrence of neuroleptic malignant syndrome (NMS) in individuals taking antipsychotic medication.

NMS is a rare but potentially fatal medication reaction involving a range of symptoms, including muscle rigidity, disorientation, irregular pulse and blood pressure, and tachycardia.

► Elderly individuals with dementia-related psychosis are at increased risk of death if treated with antipsychotic drugs and should not take Seroquel.

► There is a risk of developing hyperglycemia and diabetes mellitus in individuals treated with atypical antipsychotic medications, including Seroquel.

► Individuals taking Seroquel should be monitored closely for the potential of worsening depression or the emergence of suicidal thoughts or behavior, particularly in the early stages of medication treatment or when dosages change.

What are the dosages and forms?

The safety of Seroquel in children under the age of 18 has not been established. For the treatment of bipolar mania, the typical adult maintenance dosage of Seroquel is 400–800 mg/day, given in divided doses. For schizophrenia, the dosage may range from 150–750 mg/day. Seroquel is rapidly absorbed and reaches peak blood levels in approximately 1–2 hours. It takes 1–2 days to reach a steady state concentration in the body.

► Tablet form (AstraZeneca): 25 mg (round, peach); 50 mg (round, white); 100 mg (round, yellow); 200 mg (round, white); 300 mg (capsule-shaped, white); 400 mg (capsule-shaped, yellow). Tablets are imprinted with the word *SEROQUEL* along with the dosage strength.

From *Medication Fact Sheets: A Behavioral Medication Reference for Educators* (3rd ed.), © 2010 by D.E. Konopasek, Champaign IL: Research Press (800-519-2707, www.researchpress.com).

Sinequan is available in generic form.

What is it for?

Sinequan is a tricyclic antidepressant and is used in the treatment of major depressive disorder (MDD) and the anxiety associated with depression.

What does it do?

Sinequan has the effect of reducing anxiety and tension associated with depression, as well as improving mood, somatic symptoms, sleep, and energy. Pharmacologically, Sinequan appears to block the reuptake of norepinephrine, a central nervous system neurotransmitter.

NOTE

Pregnancy Risk Category B (no evidence of human risk; see Appendix B).

What are the side effects?

Individuals taking Sinequan may experience a wide range of side effects, including these:

1. Drowsiness
2. Urinary retention
3. Dizziness
4. Dry mouth/blurred vision
5. Blood pressure changes
6. Sweating/chills/flushing

NOTES

► It is recommended that Sinequan not be taken in combination with monoamine oxidase inhibitors (MAOIs) or within 14 days of discontinuing treatment with an MAOI. At least 14 days should be allowed after stopping Sinequan before starting an MAOI.

► Individuals with glaucoma or urinary retention should not take Sinequan.

► Individuals taking Sinequan should be monitored closely for the potential of worsening depression or the emergence of suicidal thoughts or behavior, particularly in the early stages of medication treatment or when dosages change.

What are the dosages and forms?

Sinequan is not recommended for children under the age of 12 due to a lack of research to determine the effectiveness and safety with that age group. The usual dosage for adults is 75–150 mg/day, given either singly or in divided doses. If a single daily dose is given, it is typically administered at bedtime.

► Capsule form (Pfizer): 10 mg (red cap, pink body); 25 mg (blue cap, pink body); 50 mg (pink cap, white body); 75 mg (light pink cap, white body); 100 mg (blue cap, white body); 150 mg (blue cap, blue body). Capsules are imprinted with the word *SINEQUAN*.

► Liquid form (Pfizer): Sinequan is available as an oral concentrate (10 mg/mL).

This fact sheet is not intended to cover all possible medication uses, directions, precautions, drug interactions, or adverse effects and is not a substitute for specific medical advice or to be used as a guide for prescribing.

From *Medication Fact Sheets: A Behavioral Medication Reference for Educators* (3rd ed.), © 2010 by D.E. Konopasek, Champaign IL: Research Press (800-519-2707, www.researchpress.com).

What is it for?

Strattera is used in the treatment of attention-deficit/hyperactivity disorder (ADHD).

What does it do?

Strattera is not a central nervous system stimulant, unlike most medications frequently used to treat ADHD. It appears that Strattera acts to block the reuptake of norepinephrine, a central nervous system neurotransmitter. Strattera has been shown to be useful in helping individuals improve behaviors commonly associated with ADHD, with effects such as these:

1. Improved motor activity
2. Decreased disruptiveness
3. Improved fine motor skills
4. More goal-directed behavior
5. Decreased distractibility

NOTE

Pregnancy Risk Category C (risk cannot be ruled out; see Appendix B). Strattera is not a controlled substance and there is no evidence to suggest that it can lead to physical or psychological dependence.

What are the side effects?

Individuals taking Strattera may experience a wide range of side effects, including the following:

1. Upset stomach
2. Nausea/vomiting
3. Loss of appetite
4. Dizziness
5. Fatigue
6. Mood swings

NOTES

► It is recommended that Strattera not be taken in combination with monoamine oxidase inhibitors (MAOIs) or within 14 days of discontinuing treatment with an MAOI. At least 14 days should be allowed after stopping Strattera before starting an MAOI.

► Individuals taking Strattera should be monitored closely for the potential of suicidal thoughts or behavior, particularly in the early stages of medication treatment or when dosages change.

► Strattera is not recommended for individuals with narrow-angle glaucoma.

► In rare cases, severe liver damaged has occurred in individuals taking Strattera.

► Sudden death has been reported in individuals taking Strattera who have structural heart defects or other serious heart conditions.

What are the dosages and forms?

The safety and effectiveness of Strattera in children under the age of 6 has not been determined. For children and adolescents up to 70kg (154 lb), the target daily dose is 1.2 mg/kg. Daily doses should not exceed 1.4 mg/kg, or 100 mg, whichever is less. For children over 70 kg and adults, the recommended daily dose is approximately 80 mg, typically given as a single morning dose, or divided between morning and late afternoon. Strattera is rapidly absorbed, reaching peak blood levels within 1–2 hours.

► Capsule form (Eli Lilly): 10 mg (white cap, white body); 18 mg (gold body, white cap); 25 mg (blue cap, white body); 40 mg (blue cap, blue body); 60 mg (blue cap, gold body). Capsules are imprinted with *LILLY* along with the dosage strength.

This fact sheet is not intended to cover all possible medication uses, directions, precautions, drug interactions, or adverse effects and is not a substitute for specific medical advice or to be used as a guide for prescribing.

From *Medication Fact Sheets: A Behavioral Medication Reference for Educators* (3rd ed.), © 2010 by D.E. Konopasek, Champaign IL: Research Press (800-519-2707, www.researchpress.com).

Surmontil is available in generic form.

What is it for?

Surmontil is a tricyclic antidepressant and is used in the treatment of major depressive disorder (MDD).

What does it do?

Surmontil is an antidepressant with an anxiety-reducing sedative action. It has the effect of improving mood, cognitive functioning, and concentration. The mode of action on the central nervous system is not known, although it appears to block the reuptake of norepinephrine and serotonin, central nervous system neurotransmitters. Surmontil is one of the more sedating antidepressants.

NOTE

Pregnancy Risk Category C (risk cannot be ruled out; see Appendix B).

What are the side effects?

Individuals taking Surmontil may experience a wide range of side effects, including the following:

1. Blood pressure changes
2. Dry mouth/constipation
3. Dizziness when standing up
4. Numbness/tingling/tremors
5. Nausea/vomiting
6. Perspiration/flushing

NOTES

► It is recommended that Surmontil not be taken in combination with monoamine oxidase inhibitors (MAOIs) or within 14 days of discontinuing treatment with an MAOI. At least 14 days should be allowed after stopping Surmontil before starting an MAOI.

► Individuals taking Surmontil should be monitored closely for the potential of worsening depression or the emergence of suicidal thoughts or behavior, particularly in the early stages of medication treatment or when dosages change.

What are the dosages and forms?

Surmontil is not recommended for children since its effectiveness and safety with that age group has not been established. The usual adolescent dose is 50–100 mg/day, usually given in divided doses. The usual adult dose is 75–150 mg/day. It may take 10 days to 4 weeks to obtain a therapeutic response.

► Capsule form (Odyssey): 25 mg (blue cap, yellow body); 50 mg (blue cap, orange body); 100 mg (blue cap, white body). Each capsule is imprinted with *OP*.

From *Medication Fact Sheets: A Behavioral Medication Reference for Educators* (3rd ed.), © 2010 by D.E. Konopasek, Champaign IL: Research Press (800-519-2707, www.researchpress.com).

What is it for?

Symbyax is used in the treatment of depression associated with bipolar disorder.

What does it do?

Symbyax is a combination of the antipsychotic medication olanzapine (Zyprexa) and the antidepressant fluoxetine (Prozac). It appears that Symbyax increases the availability of the neurotransmitters norepinephrine, dopamine, and serotonin, and that this increased availability appears to be responsible for the antidepressant effect.

NOTE

Pregnancy Risk Category C (risk cannot be ruled out; see Appendix B).

What are the side effects?

Individuals taking Symbyax may experience a wide range of side effects, including the following:

1. Weakness
2. Fatigue
3. Weight gain
4. Diarrhea
5. Dry mouth
6. Tardive dyskinesia/NMS

NOTE

- Tardive dyskinesia is a condition that may develop in individuals of any age group treated with antipsychotic medications for an extended period of time. Symptoms include involuntary movements of the face, tongue, mouth, or jaw and, to a lesser degree, involuntary rhythmic movements of the extremities. There is no known treatment for this condition.

- The medical literature has also reported the occurrence of neuroleptic malignant syndrome (NMS) in individuals taking antipsychotic medication. NMS is a rare but potentially fatal medication reaction involving a range of symptoms, including muscle rigidity, disorientation, irregular pulse and blood pressure, and tachycardia.

- It is recommended that Symbyax not be taken in combination with monoamine oxidase inhibitors (MAOIs) or within 14 days of discontinuing treatment with an MAOI. At least 14 days should be allowed after stopping Symbyax before starting an MAOI.

- Elderly individuals with dementia-related psychosis are at increased risk of death if treated with antipsychotic drugs and should not take Symbyax.

- Thioridazine (Mellaril) should not be taken within a minimum of 5 weeks after discontinuing Symbyax.

- There is a risk of developing hyperglycemia and diabetes mellitus in individuals treated with atypical antipsychotic medications, including olanzapine.

- Individuals taking fluoxetine should be monitored closely for the potential of worsening depression or the emergence of suicidal thoughts or behavior, particularly in the early stages of medication treatment, or when dosages change.

What are the dosages and forms?

The safety of Symbyax in children and adolescents has not been clinically established. The typical beginning adult dosage of Symbyax is the 6 mg/25 mg capsule (6 mg of olanzapine and 25 mg of fluoxetine), taken in the evening. The safety of doses above 18 mg/75 mg has not been evaluated.

- Capsule form (Eli Lilly): 3 mg/25 mg (pink cap, yellow body); 6 mg/25 mg (mustard yellow cap, light yellow body); 6 mg/50 mg (mustard yellow cap, light gray body); 12 mg/25 mg (red cap, light yellow body); 12 mg/50 mg (red cap, light gray body).

This fact sheet is not intended to cover all possible medication uses, directions, precautions, drug interactions, or adverse effects and is not a substitute for specific medical advice or to be used as a guide for prescribing.

Tegretol is available in generic form. CARBATROL, EQUETRO, and EPITOL are other brand names for carbamazepine.

What is it for?

Tegretol is an anticonvulsant medication and is useful in the treatment of psychomotor and major (grand mal) seizure disorders. It is also used to treat pain associated with trigeminal neuralgia.

What does it do?

Although the exact mechanism is unknown, it appears Tegretol depresses the thalamus and lowers the stimulation threshold in certain parts of the brain.

NOTE

Pregnancy Risk Category D (positive evidence of risk; see Appendix B).

What are the side effects?

Individuals taking Tegretol may experience a wide range of side effects, including the following:

1. Dizziness/drowsiness
2. Dry mouth
3. Vision impairments
4. Nausea/vomiting
5. Rash
6. Aplastic anemia/agranulocytosis

NOTES

► A rare but potentially fatal skin rash has been associated with individuals taking carbamazepine.

► Agranulocytosis is a rare but serious blood disorder in which the white blood cell count drops precipitously, causing a serious risk of death because of lowered resistance to infection.

► Rare occurrences of aplastic anemia (failure of the bone marrow to produce blood cells), a potentially life-threatening condition, have been reported in individuals taking Tegretol.

► Antiseizure drugs should not be discontinued abruptly due to a risk of increased seizure activity.

What are the dosages and forms?

For children under the age of 6, the maximum recommended dose for the treatment of seizure disorder is 35 mg/kg/day. For children ages 6–12, optimal dosage ranges from 400–800 mg/day. The typical adult dosage for treatment of seizures ranges from 600–1200 mg/day. With Tegretol suspension, peak blood levels occur approximately 1–2 hours after ingestion. With the tablet form, peak blood levels occur approximately 4–5 hours after ingestion. Tegretol XR reaches peak plasma levels in 3–12 hours.

► Tablet form (Novartis): 200 mg (capsule-shaped, pink). Tegretol XR (sustained-release), 100 mg (round, yellow); 200 mg (round, pink); 400 mg (round, brown). Tablets are imprinted with the letter *T* along with the dosage strength.

► Chewable tablet form (Novartis): 100 mg (round, white with pink specks).

► Liquid form (Novartis): Tegretol is available as a liquid suspension (100 mg/5 mL).

Thioridazine is available only in generic form.

What is it for?

Thioridazine is used to treat psychotic disorders. Due to serious risk of cardiac irregularities that may lead to sudden death, thioridazine should only be used to treat individuals with schizophrenia who fail to respond to other antipsychotic medications.

What does it do?

Pharmacologically, thioridazine appears to block the effects of dopamine, a central nervous system neurotransmitter. It has been shown to have a calming effect and reduces psychotic symptoms associated with schizophrenia (hallucinations and/or delusions).

NOTE

Pregnancy Risk Category C (risk cannot be ruled out; see Appendix B).

What are the side effects?

Individuals taking thioridazine may experience a wide range of side effects, including the following:

1. Drowsiness
2. Dry mouth/blurred vision
3. Tremors/restlessness
4. Constipation/diarrhea
5. Cardiac arrhythmias
6. Tardive dyskinesia/NMS

NOTES

► Thioridazine has been shown to produce serious dose-related cardiac arrhythmias that may be fatal.

► Tardive dyskinesia is a condition that may develop in individuals of any age group treated with antipsychotic medications for an extended period of time. Symptoms include involuntary movements of the face, tongue, mouth, or jaw and, to a lesser degree, involuntary rhythmic movements of the extremities. There is no known treatment for this condition.

► The medical literature has also reported the occurrence of neuroleptic malignant syndrome (NMS) in individuals taking antipsychotic medication. NMS is a rare but potentially fatal medication reaction involving a range of symptoms, including muscle rigidity, disorientation, irregular pulse and blood pressure, and tachycardia.

► Elderly individuals with dementia-related psychosis are at increased risk of death if treated with antipsychotic drugs and should not take thioridazine.

What are the dosages and forms?

For children with schizophrenia who are unresponsive to other medications, the typical dosage may range from 0.5 mg/kg/day to a maximum of 3 mg/kg/day, given in divided doses. The typical adult dose is 200–800 mg/day, given in two to four doses.

► Tablet form (Mylan): 10 mg (round, bright chartreuse); 10 mg (round, orange); 25 (round,orange); 50 mg (round, orange); 100 mg (round, orange).

► Liquid form (Actavis): Concentrate 100 mg/mL.

This fact sheet is not intended to cover all possible medication uses, directions, precautions, drug interactions, or adverse effects and is not a substitute for specific medical advice or to be used as a guide for prescribing.

Tofranil is available in generic form.

What is it for?

Tofranil is a tricyclic antidepressant and is used to treat major depressive disorder (MDD). It has also been used as a temporary treatment for childhood enuresis (bedwetting).

What does it do?

Tofranil acts to decrease irritability, stabilize mood, and decrease the highs and lows associated with some forms of depression. Pharmacologically, Tofranil appears to block the reuptake of norepinephrine, a central nervous system neurotransmitter.

NOTE

Pregnancy Risk Category D (positive evidence of risk; see Appendix B).

What are the side effects?

Individuals taking Tofranil may experience a wide range of side effects, including the following:

1. Nervousness
2. Fatigue
3. Blurred vision
4. Sleep disturbance
5. Dry mouth
6. Upset stomach

NOTES

► It is recommended that Tofranil not be taken in combination with monoamine oxidase inhibitors (MAOIs) or within 14 days of discontinuing treatment with an MAOI. At least 14 days should be allowed after stopping Tofranil before starting an MAOI.

► Individuals taking Tofranil should be monitored closely for the potential of worsening depression or the emergence of suicidal thoughts or behavior, particularly in the early stages of medication treatment or when dosages change.

What are the dosages and forms?

The usual dosage range for children over 6 years of age is 25–75 mg/day, usually given before bedtime as a treatment for enuresis. It is recommended that a daily dose of 2.5 mg/kg not be exceeded. The typical adult dosage ranges from 50–150 mg/day. It may take 1–3 weeks for the therapeutic effects of Tofranil to become evident.

► Tablet form (Mallinckrodt): 10 mg (triangular, coral); 25 mg (round, coral); 50 mg (round, coral).

► Capsule form (Mallinckrodt): Tofranil-PM, 75 mg (orange cap, orange body); 100 mg (orange cap, yellow body); 125 mg (orange cap, light yellow body); 150 mg (orange cap, orange body). Tofranil-PM should not be used in children of any age because of an increased risk of overdose due to the high potency of each capsule.

This fact sheet is not intended to cover all possible medication uses, directions, precautions, drug interactions, or adverse effects and is not a substitute for specific medical advice or to be used as a guide for prescribing.

From *Medication Fact Sheets: A Behavioral Medication Reference for Educators* (3rd ed.), © 2010 by D.E. Konopasek, Champaign IL: Research Press (800-519-2707, www.researchpress.com).

What is it for?

Topamax is an anticonvulsant as is used in the treatment of partial onset seizures and generalized tonic-clonic seizures. It is generally used in combination with other anticonvulsant medications. Topamax is also used as a treatment for migraine headaches.

What does it do?

The precise mechanism by which Topamax exerts its effects is unknown. It appears to control the spread of electrical impulses across nerve cells, thus reducing overstimulation.

NOTE

Pregnancy Risk Category C (risk cannot be ruled out; see Appendix B).

What are the side effects?

Individuals taking Topamax may experience a wide range of side effects, including the following:

1. Psychomotor slowing
2. Difficulty thinking and concentrating
3. Speech/language difficulty
4. Decreased sweating
5. Dizziness/poor balance
6. Confusion/memory problems

NOTES

- Cases of decreased bicarbonate levels (metabolic acidosis) have been associated with this medication.

- Antiseizure drugs should not be discontinued abruptly due to a risk of increased seizure activity.

- Vision changes (myopia associated with angle closure glaucoma) have been reported in individuals taking Topamax.

What are the dosages and forms?

The usual maximum daily dose of Topamax is 400 mg, given in two doses. For children ages 2–16, the typical daily dose is 5–9 mg/kg, given in two divided doses (e.g., a child weighing 80 pounds, approximately 36 kg, may receive 180–324 mg/day, given in two doses). Topamax enters the bloodstream rapidly and peaks in about 2 hours. A steady state therapeutic level is typically reached in about 4 days in individuals with normal liver function.

- Tablet form (Ortho-McNeil): 25 mg (round, white); 50 mg (round, light yellow); 100 mg (round, yellow); 200 mg (round, salmon). Tablets are embossed with the dosage strength on one side. On the reverse , *TOP* is embossed on the 25 mg tablet. *TOPAMAX* is embossed on both the 100 and 200 mg tablet.

- Capsule form (Ortho-McNeil): Topamax Sprinkles, 15 mg (off-white cap, clear body); 25 mg (off-white cap, clear body). Capsules are imprinted with *TOP* on the cap and the dosage strength on the body. Topamax Sprinkles may be taken in capsule form or opened and sprinkled on food, such as applesauce, custard, ice cream, oatmeal, pudding, or yogurt.

This fact sheet is not intended to cover all possible medication uses, directions, precautions, drug interactions, or adverse effects and is not a substitute for specific medical advice or to be used as a guide for prescribing.

TRANXENE   (Chlorazepate dipotassium)

What is it for?

Tranxene is used in the treatment of anxiety disorders. It is also used as part of the treatment of certain seizure disorders and has been used to relieve symptoms associated with alcohol withdrawal.

What does it do?

Tranxene is a central nervous system depressant and blocks the arousal of certain higher functioning brain centers, thereby exerting a calming effect. Tranxene belongs to the drug class benzodiazepine. Long-term use is not recommended.

NOTE

Tranxene is a controlled substance under DEA Schedule IV (see Appendix C). Pregnancy Risk Category D (positive evidence of risk; see Appendix B).

What are the side effects?

Individuals taking Tranxene may experience a wide range of side effects, including the following:

1. Drowsiness
2. Dizziness
3. Gastrointestinal irritation
4. Dry mouth
5. Headache
6. Mental confusion

NOTE

► Withdrawal symptoms (cramping, vomiting, convulsions, sweating, etc.) have been reported following abrupt discontinuation of Tranxene. Individuals who are prone to substance abuse/addiction should be monitored carefully when taking Tranxene due to the possibility of psychological and physiological dependence.

► Tranxene is not recommended in individuals with narrow-angle glaucoma.

What are the dosages and forms?

Tranxene is not recommended for children under the age of 9 due to a lack of clinical studies demonstrating its usefulness and safety for younger children. In adults, the typical daily dosage is 30 mg/day, given in divided doses. The maximum adult daily dose is 90 mg/day. For children ages 9–12, the maximum recommended dose is 60 mg/day, given in divided doses. Tranxene enters the bloodstream fairly quickly and exerts a therapeutic effect for approximately 2 days.

► Tablet form (Ovation): T-Tab, 3.75 mg (pyramid-shaped, light blue); 7.5 mg (pyramid-shaped, lavender); 15 mg (pyramid-shaped, pink). Each T-Tab tablet has a distinctive raised *T* embossed on the surface.

► Sustained release form (Ovation): Tranxene-SD, 22.5 mg (round, tan); Tranxene-SD Half Strength, 11.25 mg (round, blue).

From *Medication Fact Sheets: A Behavioral Medication Reference for Educators* (3rd ed.), © 2010 by D.E. Konopasek, Champaign IL: Research Press (800-519-2707, www.researchpress.com).

Trazodone is available only in generic form.

What is it for?

Trazodone is an antidepressant used in the treatment of depressive disorders. It has been found to be useful for individuals with mild to moderate depression, especially if they have difficulty falling asleep.

What does it do?

Pharmacologically, trazodone appears to block the reuptake of serotonin, a central nervous system neurotransmitter. The intended effect is an elevation of mood, improved cognitive and psychomotor functioning, and improved concentration.

NOTE

Pregnancy Risk Category C (risk cannot be ruled out; see Appendix B).

What are the side effects?

Individuals taking trazodone may experience a wide range of side effects, including the following:

1. Dry mouth
2. Sedation
3. Dizziness/fainting
4. Nausea
5. Nervousness
6. Priapism

NOTES

► Priapism is a prolonged erection in males that can cause permanent damage if not treated.

► It is recommended that trazodone not be taken in combination with monoamine oxidase inhibitors (MAOIs) or within 14 days of discontinuing treatment with an MAOI. At least 14 days should be allowed after stopping trazodone before starting an MAOI.

► Individuals taking trazodone should be monitored closely for the potential of worsening depression or the emergence of suicidal thoughts or behavior, particularly in the early stages of medication treatment or when dosages change.

What are the dosages and forms?

The safety and effectiveness of trazodone in children under the age of 18 has not been established. The typical adult dosage range is 150–300 mg daily, given in divided doses. Hospitalized patients may be given up to 600 mg/day. Trazodone enters the bloodstream quickly and reaches peak levels in approximately 1 hour. It may take several weeks for the full therapeutic effect of trazodone to be reached.

► Tablet form (various pharmaceutical companies): 50 mg; 100 mg; 150 mg.

This fact sheet is not intended to cover all possible medication uses, directions, precautions, drug interactions, or adverse effects and is not a substitute for specific medical advice or to be used as a guide for prescribing.

Stelazine is now available only as generic trifluoperazine hydrochloride.

What is it for?

Trifluoperazine is used in the management of psychotic symptoms associated with schizophrenia (hallucinations and/or delusions). It has also been used as a short-term treatment for nonpsychotic anxiety but is generally not the first drug of choice for that condition.

What does it do?

Pharmacologically, trifluoperazine seems to act by blocking the action of dopamine, a central nervous system neurotransmitter. It is moderately sedating and helps to reduce psychotic symptoms.

NOTE

Pregnancy Risk Category C (risk cannot be ruled out; see Appendix B).

What are the side effects?

Individuals taking trifluoperazine may experience a wide range of side effects, including the following:

1. Sedation/fatigue
2. Agitation/restlessness
3. Tremors/drooling
4. Hypotension/dizziness
5. Dry mouth/blurred vision
6. Tardive dyskinesia/NMS

NOTES

► Tardive dyskinesia is a condition that may develop in individuals of any age group treated with antipsychotic medications for an extended period of time. Symptoms include involuntary movements of the face, tongue, mouth, or jaw and, to a lesser degree, involuntary rhythmic movements of the extremities. There is no known treatment for this condition.

► The medical literature has also reported the occurrence of neuroleptic malignant syndrome (NMS) in individuals taking antipsychotic medication. NMS is a rare but potentially fatal medication reaction involving a range of symptoms, including muscle rigidity, disorientation, irregular pulse and blood pressure, and tachycardia.

► Elderly individuals with dementia-related psychosis are at increased risk of death if treated with antipsychotic drugs and should not take trifluoperazine.

What are the dosages and forms?

It is recommended that dosages of trifluoperazine be adjusted based on the weight of children over the age of 6. The starting dose in children is generally 1 mg, given either once or twice a day. Usually, the dosage would not exceed 15 mg/day. For adults, the effective dosage range is generally 15–20 mg/day. Optimum dosage levels may be obtained in 2–3 weeks.

► Tablet form (Mylan): 1 mg (round, white); 2 mg (round, white); 5 mg (round, lavender); 10 mg (round, lavender). Tablets are embossed with *M* on one side.

Artane is now available only as generic trihexyphenidyl.

What is it for?

Trihexyphenidyl is an antispasmodic medication used in the treatment of tremors and other Parkinsonian symptoms associated with the side-effects of some antipsychotic medications, as well as in treating symptoms of Parkinson's disease itself.

What does it do?

Trihexyphenidyl inhibits parts of the central nervous system and thereby exerts a relaxing effect on the smooth muscles.

NOTE

Pregnancy Risk Category C (risk cannot be ruled out; see Appendix B)

What are the side effects?

Individuals taking trihexyphenidyl may experience a wide range of side effects, including the following:

1. Dry mouth
2. Blurred vision
3. Dizziness
4. Mild nausea
5. Nervousness
6. Constipation

NOTE

Trihexyphenidyl is not recommended in individuals with narrow-angle glaucoma.

What are the dosages and forms?

The usual adult dosage range for trihexyphenidyl is between 5–15 mg/day, although some adults respond to as little as 1 mg/day. Trihexyphenidyl appears to be tolerated best if administered in three divided doses at mealtimes (or four doses, with the last at bedtime).

- ► Tablet form (Watson): 2 mg (round, white); 5 mg (round, white).

- ► Liquid form (various pharmaceutical companies): Trihexyphenidyl is available in elixir form (2 mg/5 mL).

From *Medication Fact Sheets: A Behavioral Medication Reference for Educators* (3rd ed.), © 2010 by D.E. Konopasek, Champaign IL: Research Press (800-519-2707, www.researchpress.com).

What is it for?

Trileptal is an anticonvulsant medication most commonly used to treat partial seizure disorders. Trileptal may either be administered alone or in conjunction with other anticonvulsant drugs.

What does it do?

Although the precise mechanism of action is not known, studies suggest Trileptal stabilizes and reduces overactive electrical impulses in the brain, which helps to prevent the spread of seizure activity.

NOTE

Pregnancy Risk Category C (risk cannot be ruled out; see Appendix B).

What are the side effects?

Individuals taking Trileptal may experience a wide range of side effects, including the following:

1. Dizziness
2. Nausea/vomiting
3. Blurred vision
4. Fatigue
5. Abdominal pain
6. Abnormal gait

NOTES

► Individuals who experience a sensitivity to carbamazapine (Tegretol) may experience similar sensitivity to Trileptal.

► Individuals taking Trileptal may develop hyponatremia (low sodium levels). Signs of hyponatremia include nausea, fatigue, headache, and/or confusion.

► Antiseizure drugs should not be discontinued abruptly due to a risk of increased seizure activity.

What are the dosages and forms?

For adults taking Trileptal, either alone or in conjunction with other anticonvulsant drugs, the recommended dose begins at 600 mg/day, administered in two doses. The maximum recommended dose is 2400 mg/day. Peak blood levels occur within 4–5 hours, and therapeutic steady state blood levels occur within 2–3 days. For children, Trileptal is typically used in conjunction with other anticonvulsant medications. The recommended dose for children ages 4–16 is based on weight. The maintenance dose for children weighing less than 29 kg is 900 mg/day. For children weighing between 29–39 kg the recommended maintenance dose is 1200 mg/day. For children weighing more than 39 kg the recommended maintenance dose is 1800 mg/day.

► Tablet form (Novartis): 150 mg (oval, pale green, imprinted with *T/D* on one side and *C/G* on the other side); 300 mg (oval, yellow, imprinted with *TE/TE* on one side and *CG/CG* on the other side); 600 mg (oval, pink, imprinted with *TF/TF* on one side and *CG/CG* on the other side). All tablets are scored on both sides.

► Liquid form (Novartis): Trileptal is available as an oral suspension (300 mg/5 mL).

From *Medication Fact Sheets: A Behavioral Medication Reference for Educators* (3rd ed.), © 2010 by D.E. Konopasek, Champaign IL: Research Press (800-519-2707, www.researchpress.com).

Valium is available in generic form.

What is it for?

Valium is used in the short-term treatment of anxiety or tension associated with stress. It has also been used as a short-term treatment for muscle spasms and as a part of the treatment for agitation and tremors associated with alcohol withdrawal.

What does it do?

Valium is a central nervous system depressant and belongs to the drug class benzodiazepine. Valium seems to affect parts of the limbic system of the brain, thalamus, and hypothalamus, thereby exerting a calming effect.

NOTE

Valium is a controlled substance under DEA Schedule IV (see Appendix C). Pregnancy Risk Category D (positive evidence of risk; see Appendix B).

What are the side effects?

Individuals taking Valium may experience a wide range of side effects, including the following:

1. Drowsiness
2. Confusion
3. Constipation
4. Fatigue
5. Depression
6. Dizziness

NOTE

Withdrawal symptoms (cramping, vomiting, convulsions, sweating, etc.) have been reported following abrupt discontinuation of Valium. Individuals who are prone to substance abuse/addiction should be monitored carefully when taking Valium due to the possibility for psychological and physiological dependence.

What are the dosages and forms?

The maximum adult daily dosage for Valium is approximately 40 mg/day. For children above 6 months of age, the maximum daily dosage may reach 10 mg/day, usually given in three to four divided doses. Valium is absorbed fairly quickly, reaching a peak plasma concentration in approximately 1–2 hours.

- Tablet form (Roche): 2 mg (round with a perforated *V*, white); 5 mg (round with a perforated *V*, yellow); 10 mg (round with a perforated *V*, blue).

- Liquid form (Roxane): Diazepam is available as an oral solution and as a concentrate.

- Injectable form (various pharmaceutical companies): Diazepam is available as an intramuscular injection (10 mg/2 mL).

- Suppository form (Valeant): Diazepam is available as a rectal suppository gel under the trade name Diastat Acudial (5.0 mg/mL).

This fact sheet is not intended to cover all possible medication uses, directions, precautions, drug interactions, or adverse effects and is not a substitute for specific medical advice or to be used as a guide for prescribing.

From *Medication Fact Sheets: A Behavioral Medication Reference for Educators* (3rd ed.), © 2010 by D.E. Konopasek, Champaign IL: Research Press (800-519-2707, www.researchpress.com).

Vistaril is available in generic form.

What is it for?

Vistaril is an antihistamine medication used as a short-term treatment for anxiety disorders and agitation. It has also been used as a preoperative sedative.

What does it do?

Although Vistaril is not chemically a depressant, it seems to suppress certain key areas of the central nervous system. It also appears to have the effect of relaxing skeletal muscles.

NOTE

Pregnancy Risk Category C (risk cannot be ruled out; see Appendix B).

What are the side effects?

Individuals taking Vistaril may experience a wide range of side effects, including the following:

1. Drowsiness
2. Dry mouth
3. Tremors
4. Dizziness
5. Headache
6. Nausea/vomiting

NOTE

Vistaril can have an additive effect if taken with central nervous system depressants (e.g., narcotics, barbiturates).

What are the dosages and forms?

The typical dosage for children under 6 years of age is 50 mg/day given in divided doses. For children over 6 years of age and adults, the dosage ranges between 50–100 mg/day. Vistaril is rapidly absorbed into the bloodstream and reaches a peak level in about 15–30 minutes.

► Capsule form (Pfizer): 25 mg (dark green cap, light green body); 50 mg (dark green cap, white body).

► Liquid form (Pfizer): Vistrail is also available as an oral suspension (25 mg/5mL).

This fact sheet is not intended to cover all possible medication uses, directions, precautions, drug interactions, or adverse effects and is not a substitute for specific medical advice or to be used as a guide for prescribing.

From *Medication Fact Sheets: A Behavioral Medication Reference for Educators* (3rd ed.), © 2010 by D.E. Konopasek, Champaign IL: Research Press (800-519-2707, www.researchpress.com).

Vivactil is available in generic form.

What is it for?

Vivactil is a tricyclic antidepressant used to treat major depressive disorder (MDD) in individuals who are under close medical supervision. Due to the activating properties of protriptyline, patients may be at an increased risk for suicide in the early stages of treatment.

What does it do?

Vivactil is an activating antidepressant. It has the effect of improving mood, somatic symptoms, sleep, and energy.

NOTE

Pregnancy Risk Category C (risk cannot be ruled out; see Appendix B).

What are the side effects?

Individuals taking Vivactil may experience a wide range of side effects, including the following:

1. Dizziness when standing up
2. Headache
3. Fatigue
4. Dry mouth, blurred vision
5. Nausea/vomiting
6. Irregular heartbeat

NOTE

► It is recommended that Vivactil not be taken in combination with monoamine oxidase inhibitors (MAOIs) or within 14 days of discontinuing treatment with an MAOI. At least 14 days should be allowed after stopping Vivactil before starting an MAOI.

► Individuals taking Vivactil should be monitored closely for the potential of worsening depression or the emergence of suicidal thoughts or behavior, particularly in the early stages of medication treatment or when dosages change.

What are the dosages and forms?

Vivactil is not recommended for children under 12 years of age due to a lack of research demonstrating its effectiveness and safety with that age group. The typical adolescent dose begins with 5 mg given three times a day (15 mg/day). The usual adult dosage range is 15–40 mg/day.

► Tablet form (Odyssey): 5 mg (oval, orange); 10 mg (oval, yellow).

This fact sheet is not intended to cover all possible medication uses, directions, precautions, drug interactions, or adverse effects and is not a substitute for specific medical advice or to be used as a guide for prescribing.

What is it for?

Vyvanse is used in the treatment of attention-deficit/hyerpactivity disorder (ADHD) in both children and adults.

What does it do?

Vyvanse is a central nervous system stimulant. It is thought to block the reuptake of norepinephine and dopamine. Stimulants have been shown to be useful in helping individuals improve behaviors commonly associated with ADHD, with effects such as these:

1. More controlled motor activity
2. Decreased disruptiveness
3. Improved concentration
4. Improved fine motor coordination
5. More goal-directed behavior
6. Decreased distractibility
7. Improved voice modulation

NOTE

Vyvanse is a controlled substance under DEA Schedule II (high potential for abuse; see Appendix C). Pregnancy Risk Category C (risk cannot be ruled out; see Appendix B).

What are the side effects?

Individuals taking Vyvanse may experience a wide range of side effects, including the following:

1. Nausea/upset stomach
2. Headache
3. Loss of appetite
4. Irritability
5. Dry mouth
6. Insomnia

NOTES

► Sudden death has been reported in individuals taking stimulant medications who have structural heart defects or other serious heart conditions.

► Medical literature reports that stimulants may intensify the motor and/or vocal tics characteristic of Tourette's syndrome.

► Individuals taking stimulant medications should not take monoamine oxidase inhibitors (MAOIs) at the same time or within 14 days of discontinuing treatment with an MAOI.

What are the dosages and forms?

The effectiveness or safety of Vyvanse has not been studied in children under the age of 6 or in adolescents over the age of 12. The recommended dosage for children ages 6–12 is 30–70 mg, given as a single dose in the morning. Vyvanse is rapidly absorbed, with peak blood levels occurring within approximately 1 hour after ingestion.

► Capsule form (Shire): 20 mg (ivory cap, ivory body); 30 mg (orange cap, white body); 40 mg (blue green cap, white body); 50 mg (blue cap, white body); 60 mg (aqua cap, aqua body); 70 mg (orange cap, blue body).

This fact sheet is not intended to cover all possible medication uses, directions, precautions, drug interactions, or adverse effects and is not a substitute for specific medical advice or to be used as a guide for prescribing.

Wellbutrin is available in generic form.

What is it for?

Wellbutrin is an antidepressant used in the treatment of major depressive disorder (MDD). It has also been used as a second-line treatment for attention-deficit/hyperactivity disorder (ADHD).

What does it do?

Pharmacologically, Wellbutrin impedes the reabsorption of serotonin, norepinephrine, and dopamine, all central nervous system neurotransmitters. It has the effect of improving mood, somatic symptoms, sleep patterns, and energy.

NOTE

Pregnancy Risk Category B (no evidence of risk in humans; see Appendix B).

What are the side effects?

Individuals taking Wellbutrin may experience a wide range of side effects, including the following:

1. Agitation
2. Tremor
3. Insomnia
4. Headache/migraine
5. Nausea/vomiting
6. Skin rash

NOTES

► It is recommended that Wellbutrin not be taken in combination with monoamine oxidase inhibitors (MAOIs) or within 14 days of discontinuing treatment with an MAOI. At least 14 days should be allowed after stopping Wellbutrin before starting an MAOI.

► There is some evidence that Wellbutrin may cause seizures (incidence at 4 per 1,000 at a dose of 400 mg/day).

► Patients should be cautioned against taking Wellbutrin in combination with the smoking cessa-tion product Zyban since both contain the active ingredient bupropion.

► Individuals taking Wellbutrin should be monitored closely for the potential of worsening depression or the emergence of suicidal thoughts or behavior, particularly in the early stages of medication treatment or when dosages change.

What are the dosages and forms?

The usefulness and safety of Wellbutrin for children under the age of 18 has not been clinically determined. The usual daily adult dosage is 300 mg/day, divided into three doses for the regular form (two doses for Wellbutrin SR, one dose for Wellbutrin XL). Peak blood levels of Wellbutrin occur within 2 hours of ingestion and remain at therapeutic level for approximately 14 hours. It may take up to 4 weeks for the full therapeutic effects of Wellbutrin to become apparent.

► Tablet form (GlaxoSmithKline): 75 mg (round, yellow); 100 mg (round, red). Wellbutrin SR (sustained release) peak blood levels occur approximately 3 hours after ingestion, 100 mg (round, blue); 150 mg (round, purple); 200 mg (round, pink). Wellbutrin is also available in extended release form as Wellbutrin XL, 150 mg (round, pale yellow); 300 mg (round, pale yellow).

From *Medication Fact Sheets: A Behavioral Medication Reference for Educators* (3rd ed.), © 2010 by D.E. Konopasek, Champaign IL: Research Press (800-519-2707, www.researchpress.com).

XANAX   (Alprazolam)

Xanax is available in generic form.

What is it for?

Xanax is an antianxiety medication used in the short-term treatment of anxiety and hypertension as well as panic disorder. It has also been used for anxiety associated with depression, generalized anxiety disorder (GAD), and panic disorder.

What does it do?

Xanax is a central nervous system depressant and thereby exerts a calming effect. It belongs to the drug class benzodiazepine. Long-term use is not recommended.

NOTE

Xanax is a controlled substance under DEA Schedule IV (see Appendix C). Pregnancy Risk Category D (positive evidence of risk; see Appendix B).

What are the side effects?

Individuals taking Xanax may experience a wide range of side effects, including the following:

1. Drowsiness
2. Impaired coordination
3. Fatigue
4. Irritability
5. Lightheadedness/dizziness
6. Increased appetite

NOTES

► Withdrawal symptoms (cramping, vomiting, convulsions, sweating, etc.) have been reported following abrupt discontinuation of Xanax. Individuals who are prone to substance abuse/addiction should be monitored carefully when taking Xanax due to the possibility for psychological and physiological dependence.

► Individuals with narrow-angle glaucoma should not take Xanax.

What are the dosages and forms?

The typical dosage range for adults taking Xanax is 1–6 mg/day, given in divided doses (once-a-day dosing for Xanax XR). The safety and usefulness of Xanax in children under the age of 18 has not been determined. Peak blood levels of Xanax occur within about 1–2 hours after ingestion (Xanax XR has a slower absorption rate), maintaining a therapeutic blood level for approximately 11 hours.

► Tablet form (Pharmacia): 0.25 mg (oval, white); 0.5 mg (oval, peach); 1 mg (oval, blue); 2 mg (oblong, scored in fourths, white). Tablets have the word *XANAX* imprinted on the surface. Xanax is available in extended release form as Xanax XR, 0.5 mg (pentagonal, white); 1 mg (square, yellow); 2 mg (round, blue); 3 mg (triangular, green).

► Alprazolam is also available in orally disintegrating tablet form under the trade name NIRAVAM (Schwarz), 0.25 mg (round, yellow); 0.5 mg (round yellow); 1 mg (round white); 2 mg (round, white).

This fact sheet is not intended to cover all possible medication uses, directions, precautions, drug interactions, or adverse effects and is not a substitute for specific medical advice or to be used as a guide for prescribing.

From *Medication Fact Sheets: A Behavioral Medication Reference for Educators* (3rd ed.), © 2010 by D.E. Konopasek, Champaign IL: Research Press (800-519-2707, www.researchpress.com).

Zarontin is available in generic form.

What is it for?

Zarontin is an anticonvulsant medication and is used in the treatment of absence (petit mal) seizure disorders.

What does it do?

Zarontin seems to suppress certain brain wave activity associated with lapses of consciousness, common to absence seizures.

NOTE

Pregnancy Risk Category C (risk cannot be ruled out; see Appendix B).

What are the side effects?

Individuals taking Zarontin may experience a wide range of side effects, including the following:

1. Decreased appetite
2. Stomach upset
3. Diarrhea
4. Drowsiness
5. Headache
6. Irritability

NOTES

► Cases of blood dyscrasias (imbalance of blood constituents) have been reported among patients taking Zarontin. Therefore, periodic blood counts are recommended.

► Antiseizure drugs should not be discontinued abruptly due to a risk of increased seizure activity.

What are the dosages and forms?

The optimal dose for most children ages 3–6 is 250 mg/day. For children ages 6 and older, the recommended maximum dose is 500 mg/day. The optimal dosage for most children is 20 mg/kg/day. Dosage increases of 250 mg every 4–7 days are typical until the desired therapeutic effect is reached. Daily divided doses of over 1.5 grams should occur only under very strict medical supervision. Zarontin may be administered in combination with other anticonvulsant medications if other types of seizures exist along with absence seizures.

► Capsule form (Parke-Davis): 250 mg (amber capsule).

► Liquid form (Parke-Davis): Zarontin is also available as a syrup (250 mg/5 mL).

This fact sheet is not intended to cover all possible medication uses, directions, precautions, drug interactions, or adverse effects and is not a substitute for specific medical advice or to be used as a guide for prescribing.

From *Medication Fact Sheets: A Behavioral Medication Reference for Educators* (3rd ed.), © 2010 by D.E. Konopasek, Champaign IL: Research Press (800-519-2707, www.researchpress.com).

Zoloft is available in generic form.

What is it for?

Zoloft is an antidepressant and is used in the treatment of major depressive disorder (MDD). It has also been used to treat obsessive-compulsive disorder (OCD), panic disorder, social anxiety disorder, posttraumatic stress disorder (PTSD), and premenstrual dysphoric disorder (PMDD).

What does it do?

Zoloft belongs to a group of antidepressants known as selective serotonin reuptake inhibitors (SSRIs). As such, it acts to block or inhibit the reabsorption of serotonin, a central nervous system neurotransmitter. The intended effect is an elevation of mood, improved cognitive and psychomotor functioning, and improved concentration.

NOTE

Pregnancy Risk Category C (risk cannot be ruled out; see Appendix B).

What are the side effects?

Individuals taking Zoloft may experience a wide range of side effects, including the following:

1. Nausea/diarrhea
2. Tremors/shakiness
3. Increased sweating
4. Decreased libido
5. Drowsiness/fatigue
6. Dry mouth

NOTES

- It is recommended that Zoloft not be taken in combination with monoamine oxidase inhibitors (MAOIs) or within 14 days of discontinuing treatment with an MAOI. At least 14 days should be allowed after stopping Zoloft before starting an MAOI.

- A serious, potentially life-threatening condition known as serotonin syndrome can occur when SSRIs and certain medications used to treat migraine headaches (triptans) are taken together.

- Zoloft should not be taken in combination with the antipsychotic drug Orap (pimozide).

- Individuals taking Zoloft should be monitored closely for the potential of worsening depression or the emergence of suicidal thoughts or behavior, particularly in the early stages of medication treatment or when dosages change.

What are the dosages and forms?

Depending upon the condition being treated, the typical dosage range for Zoloft is 25–200 mg/day, usually given in a single dose, either in the morning or evening. Peak blood levels of Zoloft usually occur within 4–8 hours. It may take a week or more for a stable plasma level to be reached.

- Tablet form (Pfizer): 25 mg (elongated, green); 50 mg (elongated, light blue); 100 mg (elongated, light yellow). Tablets are imprinted with the word *ZOLOFT* along with the dosage strength.

- Liquid form (Pfizer): Zoloft is available as a liquid concentrate (20 mg/mL).

This fact sheet is not intended to cover all possible medication uses, directions, precautions, drug interactions, or adverse effects and is not a substitute for specific medical advice or to be used as a guide for prescribing.

From *Medication Fact Sheets: A Behavioral Medication Reference for Educators* (3rd ed.), © 2010 by D.E. Konopasek, Champaign IL: Research Press (800-519-2707, www.researchpress.com).

What is it for?

Zyprexa is used to treat schizophrenia. It has been used as a treatment for manic episodes of Bipolar I disorder, either alone or in combination with lithium or valproate (Depacon). The intramuscular injection form of Zyprexa has been used to treat agitation associated with schizophrenia or Bipolar I mania.

What does it do?

Zyprexa has the effect of diminishing the symptoms of schizophrenia by reducing psychotic symptoms (delusions and hallucinations), in addition to improving cognitive functioning and mood. Pharmacologically, Zyprexa appears to block the central nervous system neurotransmitters dopamine and serotonin.

NOTE

Pregnancy Risk Category C (risk cannot be ruled out; see Appendix B).

What are the side effects?

Individuals taking Zyprexa may experience a wide range of side effects, including the following:

1. Dizziness when standing up
2. Drowsiness
3. Tremors/shakiness
4. Upset stomach
5. Weight gain
6. Tardive dyskinesia/NMS

NOTES

► Tardive dyskinesia is a condition that may develop in individuals of any age group treated with antipsychotic medications for an extended period of time. Symptoms include involuntary movements of the face, tongue, mouth, or jaw and, to a lesser degree, involuntary rhythmic movements of the extremities. There is no known treatment for this condition.

► The medical literature has also reported the occurrence of neuroleptic malignant syndrome (NMS) in individuals taking antipsychotic medication. NMS is a rare but potentially fatal medication reaction involving a range of symptoms, including muscle rigidity, disorientation, irregular pulse and blood pressure, and tachycardia.

► Elderly individuals with dementia-related psychosis are at increased risk of death if treated with antipsychotic drugs and should not take Zyprexa.

► There is a risk of developing hyperglycemia and diabetes mellitus in individuals treated with atypical antipsychotic medications, including Zyprexa.

What are the dosages and forms?

The safety of Zyprexa in children under the age of 18 has not been clinically established. The typical adult dosage range of Zyprexa is 10–15 mg/day, administered in a single dose. Zyprexa is well-absorbed and reaches peak plasma levels approximately 6 hours after administration. It may take 7–10 days for the full therapeutic effects of Zyprexa to become apparent.

► Tablet form (Eli Lilly): 2.5 mg (round, white); 5 mg (round, white); 7.5 mg (round, white); 10 mg (round, white); 15 mg (elliptical, blue); 20 mg (elliptical, pink). Tablets are imprinted with the word *LILLY.* An orally-disintegrating form of Zyprexa, Zyprexa Zydis, is available in 5.0 mg, 10 mg, 15 mg, and 20 mg tablets (round, yellow). Zyprexa Zydis begins dissolving immediately in the mouth and may be taken with or without liquid.

► Injection form (Eli Lilly): Zyprexa is available as an intramuscular injection (10 mg).

This fact sheet is not intended to cover all possible medication uses, directions, precautions, drug interactions, or adverse effects and is not a substitute for specific medical advice or to be used as a guide for prescribing.

Medications by Class

Antianxiety, Antihypertensives, and Minor Tranquilizers

Ativan

BuSpar

Catapres

Dalmane

Diovan

Doral

Halcion

Inderal

Klonopin

Librium

Limbitrol

Meprobamate

Oxazepam

Restoril

Tranxene

Valium

Xanax

Anticonvulsants

Celontin

Depakene

Dilantin

Felbatol

Gabitril

Lamictal

Mebaral

Mysoline

Neurontin

Phenobarbital

Tegretol

Topamax

Trileptal

Zarontin

Antidepressants

Amitriptyline

Amoxapine

Anafranil

Celexa

Cymbalta

Effexor

Lexapro

Lithium (mood stabilizer)

Luvox

Marplan (MAO inhibitor)

Nardil (MAO inhibitor)

Nefazodone

Norpramin

Pamelor

Parnate (MAO inhibitor)

Paxil

Pristiq

Prozac

Remeron

Sinequan

Surmontil

Symbyax (mood stabilizer)

Tofranil

Trazodone

Vivactil

Wellbutrin

Zoloft

Antipsychotics

Abilify

Chlorpromazine

Clozaril

Fluphenazine

Geodon

Haldol

Invega

Loxapine

Moban

Navane

Orap

Perphenazine

Prochlorpromazine

Risperdal

Seroquel

Thioridazine

Trifluoperazine

Zyprexa

Antihistamines, Medications for Side Effects

Benadryl

Cogentin

Eldepryl (MAO inhibitor)

Trihexyphenidyl

Vistaril

Stimulants

Adderall

Concerta

Daytrana

Desoxyn

Dexedrine

Focalin

Metadate

Methylin

Ritalin

Strattera (nonstimulant ADHD medication)

Vyvanse

Appendix B

FDA Pregnancy Risk Categories

The Food and Drug Administration (FDA) categorizes medications according to their potential risk in pregnant women. Medications are ranked from relatively low pregnancy risk (A) to high pregnancy risk (X).

A: CONTROLLED STUDIES SHOW NO RISK

Adequate studies in pregnant women have not demonstrated a risk to the fetus in the first trimester of pregnancy, and there is no evidence of risk in later trimesters.

B: NO EVIDENCE OF RISK IN HUMANS

(1) Animal studies have not demonstrated a risk to the fetus, but there are no adequate studies in pregnant women or (2) animal studies have shown an adverse effect, but adequate studies in pregnant women have not demonstrated a risk to the fetus during the first trimester of pregnancy, and there is no evidence of risk in later trimesters.

C: RISK CANNOT BE RULED OUT

(1) Animal studies have shown an adverse effect on the fetus, but there are no adequate studies in humans; the benefits of the drug in pregnant women may be acceptable despite its potential risks or (2) there are no animal reproduction studies and no adequate studies in humans.

D: POSITIVE EVIDENCE OF RISK

There is evidence of human fetal risk, but the potential benefits from the use of the drug in pregnant women may be acceptable despite its potential risks.

X: CONTRAINDICATED IN PREGNANCY

(1) Studies in animals or humans demonstrate fetal abnormalities or (2) adverse reaction reports indicate evidence of fetal risk. The risk of use in a pregnant woman clearly outweighs any possible benefit.

Appendix C

DEA Controlled Substance Schedule

Under the Controlled Substances Act of 1970, many drugs are designated as controlled substances due to their potential for abuse. The Drug Enforcement Administration (DEA) provides a ranking, or schedule, of controlled drugs based on their abuse potential. These drug categories are ranked from Schedule I (high abuse potential) to Schedule V (low abuse potential).

Schedule I

(A) The drug has a high potential for abuse.

(B) The drug has no currently accepted medical use in treatment in the United States.

(C) There is a lack of accepted safety for use of the drug under medical supervision.

Examples: LSD, peyote, mescaline, psilocybin, THC, MDA, heroin.

Schedule II

(A) The drug has a high potential for abuse.

(B) The drug has a currently accepted medical use in treatment in the United States or a currently accepted medical use with severe restrictions.

(C) Abuse of the drug may lead to severe psychological or physical dependence.

Examples: Opium, morphine, amphetamines, methylphenidate.

Schedule III

(A) The drug has a potential for abuse less than the drugs in Schedules I and II.

(B) The drug has a currently accepted medical use in the United States.

(C) Abuse of the drug may lead to moderate or low physical dependence or high psychological dependence.

Examples: Glutethimide, methyprylon, nalorphine, codeine.

Schedule IV

(A) The drug has a low potential for abuse relative to the drugs in Schedule III.

(B) The drug has a currently accepted medical use in treatment in the United States.

(C) Abuse of the drug may lead to limited physical dependence or psychological dependence relative to the drugs in Schedule III.

Examples: Phenobarbital, meprobamate, fenfluramine, diazepam.

Schedule V

(A) The drug has a low potential for abuse relative to the drugs in Schedule IV.

(B) The drug has a currently accepted medical use in treatment in the United States.

(C) Abuse of the drug may lead to limited physical dependence or psychological dependence relative to the drugs in Schedule IV.

Examples: Preparations containing limited quantities of certain narcotic drugs, generally for antitussive or antidiarrheal purposes.

Appendix D
Glossary of Pharmacological Terms

a.c.	before meals	NR	do not refill
a.m., A.M.	morning	o.d.	once a day
aq	water	p.c.	after meals
aq dist.	distilled water	po, p.o., PO	by mouth
ASA	aspirin	PR	by rectum
b.i.d.	two times per day	p.r.n., PRN	when needed or necessary
b.i.n.	two times per night	q.d.	every day
caps, Caps	capsule(s)	q.h.	every hour
DEA	Drug Enforcement Administration	q2hr	every 2 hours
elix	elixir	q3hr	every 3 hours
emuls.	emulsion	q4hr	every 4 hours
FDA	Food and Drug Administration	qhs	every night
g, gm	gram (1000 mg)	q.i.d.	four times a day
GABA	gamma-aminobutyric acid	qmo	every month
gr	grain	q.o.d.	every other day
gtt	a drop, drops	q.s.	as much as needed, quantity sufficient
h, hr	hour	Rx	prescription symbol
h.s.	at bedtime	sc, SC, SQ	subcutaneous
im, IM	intramuscular	sol	solution
iv, IV	intravenous	SR	sustained release
kg	kilogram (2.2 lb)	stat	immediately, first dose
l, L	liter (1,000 mL)	syr	syrup
MAO	monoamine oxidase	tab	tablet
mcg	microgram	t.i.d.	three times per day
mEq	milliequivalent	t.i.n.	three times per night
mg	milligram	ung	ointment
mL	milliliter	ut dict	as directed
NPO	nothing by mouth	vit	vitamin

Bibliography

Books and Articles

Forness, S. R., Walker, H. M., & Kavale, K. A. (2003–2004, Winter). Psychiatric disorders and their treatment: A primer for teachers. *Teaching Exceptional Children, 36*(2), 42–49.

Julien, R. M. (2004). *A primer of drug action (10th ed.)*. New York: Worth Publishers.

Konopasek, D. E., & Forness, S. R. (2004). Research regarding the use of psychopharmacology in the treatment of emotional and behavioral disorders. In R. B. Rutherford, M. M. Quinn, & S. R. Mathur (Eds.), *Handbook of Research in Behavioral Disorders*. New York: Guilford.

Schoenfeld, N., & Konopasek, D. E. (2007). Medicine in the classroom: A review of psychiatric medications for students with emotional or behavioral disorders. *Beyond Behavior, 17*(1), 14–20.

Wilens, T. (2008) *Straight talk about psychiatric medications for kids (3rd ed.)*. New York: Guilford.

Websites

Anxiety Disorders Association of America (ADAA): **www.adaa.org**

This site provides links to specific anxiety disorders, including prevalence statistics, diagostic information, and treatment options.

Attention Deficit Disorder Association (ADDA): **www.add.org**

Explore this site for information related to ADHD

Centers for Disease Control and Prevention (CDC): **www.cdc.gov**

The CDC website has links to a wide variety of health related topics. You can click on "Diseases and Conditions" to link to a full spectrum of both physical and psychiatric conditions, with further links that address treatment issues.

Mental Health America (MHA): **www.mentalhealthamerica.net**

This site provides links to a long list of mental health issues, including statistics, diagnostic information, and treatment options.

National Alliance on Mental Illness (NAMI): **www.nami.org/Hometemplate.cfm**

Click on the "Inform Yourself" link to "About Medication" for more information regarding psychiatric medications. Explore the NAMI site to learn more about mental illness.

National Institute of Mental Health (NIMH). **www.nimh.nih.gov**

Click on "Publications." You will find this link provides a wealth of information on all topics related to mental health, including statistics, diagnosis, and treatment.

Index

Bold face text represents brand-name medications.

About the Author

Dean E. Konopasek received his Ph.D. in special education at Utah State University in 1976 and is currently chair of the Department of Counseling and Special Education at the University of Alaska Anchorage. His professional interest in issues surrounding psychiatric medications began following graduate school when he became principal of the inpatient school at the Alaska Psychiatric Institute in Anchorage. Observing that teachers, counselors, psychologists, and other nonmedical professionals often had little knowledge regarding the uses and effects (both intended effects and side effects) of psychiatric drugs, Dr. Konopasek developed the initial version of *Medication Fact Sheets* in 1994. The book has been revised many times between then and publication of this most recent edition.